# The Efficient Library

# The Efficient Library

## Ten Simple Changes That Save Time and Improve Service

Elizabeth Barrera Rush

An Imprint of ABC-CLIO, LLC
Santa Barbara, California • Denver, Colorado

Copyright © 2020 Elizabeth Barrera Rush

All rights reserved. No part of this publication may be reproduced, stored in a retrieval system, or transmitted, in any form or by any means, electronic, mechanical, photocopying, recording, or otherwise, except for the inclusion of brief quotations in a review, without prior permission in writing from the publisher.

**Library of Congress Cataloging-in-Publication Data**

Names: Rush, Elizabeth Barrera, author.
Title: The efficient library : ten simple changes that save time and improve service / Elizabeth Barrera Rush.
Description: Santa Barbara, California : Libraries Unlimited, [2020] | Includes bibliographical references and index.
Identifiers: LCCN 2020005636 (print) | LCCN 2020005637 (ebook) | ISBN 9781440869815 (paperback ; acid-free paper) | ISBN 9781440869822 (ebook)
Subjects: LCSH: Library administration—United States. | Library administration—United States—Case studies. | Libraries—Self-evaluation—United States. | Libraries—Space utilization—United States. | Public services (Libraries)—United States. | Librarians—Time management—United States.
Classification: LCC Z678 .R797 2020 (print) | LCC Z678 (ebook) | DDC 025.1—dc23
LC record available at https://lccn.loc.gov/2020005636
LC ebook record available at https://lccn.loc.gov/2020005637

ISBN: 978-1-4408-6981-5 (paperback)
    978-1-4408-6982-2 (ebook)

24  23  22  21  20      1  2  3  4  5

This book is also available as an eBook.

Libraries Unlimited
An Imprint of ABC-CLIO, LLC

ABC-CLIO, LLC
147 Castilian Drive
Santa Barbara, California 93117
www.abc-clio.com

This book is printed on acid-free paper ∞

Manufactured in the United States of America

# Contents

*Acknowledgments*   vii

*Introduction*   ix

**Part One**   **Creating an Efficient Library**

**Chapter 1**   Regain Your Evenings and Weekends   3

**Chapter 2**   How to Become the Best Evaluator of What You Do   9

**Chapter 3**   Addressing Fears and Misconceptions of What Efficiency Will Bring   15

**Chapter 4**   Wise Uses of Newfound Time   21

**Part Two**   **Ten Simple Changes**

**Chapter 5**   Change #1: Organize Your Desk   29

**Chapter 6**   Change #2: Analyze Daily Routines   39

**Chapter 7**   Change #3: Create Routines for Purchasing and Receiving   65

**Chapter 8**   Change #4: Create a Receiving, Processing, Repair Station   81

**Chapter 9**   Change #5: Implement Procedures for Effective Communication   87

**Chapter 10**   Change #6: Manage Storage and Reordering of Supplies   97

| | | |
|---|---|---|
| **Chapter 11** | Change #7: Analyze Causes of Stressors and Take Precautions | 101 |
| **Chapter 12** | Change #8: Weed and Clear the Library Space | 115 |
| **Chapter 13** | Change #9: Reconfigure the Library Space | 123 |
| **Chapter 14** | Change #10: Prepare for Refurnishing, Renovating, Remodeling, or New Construction | 141 |
| Conclusion | | 155 |
| *Index* | | 157 |

# Acknowledgments

It is quite a privilege to be able to honor and thank the people who are essentially a part of this book.

Everyone whose keen eyes have worked on the text of this book, including Michelle Scott, Emma Bailey, and Nitesh Sharma, made the writing process manageable and enjoyable, and I am especially thankful for Sharon Coatney, who warms my heart when she refers to me as "one of her authors," and that she has faith in my ideas.

Blanche Woolls, my library management inspiration and hero, whose books helped me build a solid foundation for my career in my early years as a librarian and through her words inspired me to pursue continuous self-improvement in order to better serve the people in each library that I had the pleasure of working in.

I am thankful for librarians Olga Barreto, Francie Ingram, and Genevieve Orozco, at Northside Independent School District in San Antonio. Each of these brave and daring librarians were ready and willing to implement my ideas or techniques to make positive changes in their space. I am also very honored that there were other librarians who shared their stories so candidly, that they have allowed me to share their stories with you, and that they were willing to share their experiences without recognition. Their stories were essential to bring warmth and humanness to this book. I am also grateful to Nicki Stohr, director of the Wilson County Public Library in Floresville, Texas, and Carolyn Foote, Westlake High School in Austin, Texas, for sharing their experiences and joys of the process of library renovations.

Above all, there is my family: chosen and by birth. The family I choose is my dear friend Greg Gonzales, who introduced me to the concepts of industrial engineering and process management and helped me find the time to grow with new life in my career as an experienced librarian.

And there is the family that has been an essential part of both my personal and professional life. These are the people who, in our everyday conversations, have provided me with seeds of knowledge that I planted, grew, and placed in my landscape of library experiences. My husband Robert, the love of my life, who not only discussed some of the legal issues with me but also devotedly cared for everyone and everything around me that was ignored while I spent evenings, weekends, and holidays writing this book. My adult children, Elise and Bobby, who have shared their experiences in public health and engineering, and give me so much pride in their accomplishments. My parents, Gil and Norma Barrera, who, by example, taught all of their children to think, create, and passionately apply their natural talents in both life and work. My brothers, Gilbert C. Barrera Jr. and Norman C. Barrera, who generously shared their perspectives of accounting and architecture over the years and in the work of this book; and my sister, Irene Rose Casas, whose love and life will always remind me just how precious time is, and to never, ever waste it.

# Introduction

I have a problem. Everywhere I go, I notice how work environments are set up and how the people are operating inside of them.

My husband's mother was a professional waitress; his brother has spent his entire life working in, managing, and owning restaurants; and my husband, Robert, after his day job as an attorney, spends his evenings and weekends being my personal chef. As the embodiment of the word "foodie," he also loves to take me to dine out, not just to enjoy a meal that he didn't prepare, but to scrutinize the ingredients and how it was created so we can appreciate the perfection of or identify the flaws in the atmosphere, and even more importantly, to judge the service. One might say we are "wannabe food critics," or that we treat eating out as entertainment as well as a quest for uniquely prepared cuisine. So when we're at restaurants, if I can see into the kitchen, I have been trained to admire a smoothly operating machine of chefs and their tools within reach; the staff flowing, facilitating, and expediting; servers at the ready, taking plates out to happy customers who are ready to partake. Likewise, I also have been taught to identify a kitchen that is in a terrible state of disarray. When I see the wait staff aimlessly bouncing about the restaurant, looking extremely busy, I know then to turn my attention to the customers. If there are tables still waiting for meals, customer faces reveal mounting impatience and anger as the hustle-bustle of wait staff produce no results. It becomes evident that the organization and management are weak. And for me, this experience morphs in my imagination into an episode of *Hell's Kitchen* or *Hell's Nightmare*! I cringe when I imagine Chef Gordon Ramsay bursting through the door, yelling at people and calling them names. He's shaming the entire restaurant staff, including the owner.

I experience this with libraries.

When I enter a library, the first thing I notice is the circulation desk—not to judge the librarian, but to assess the climate in which the people are functioning. I observe the size and amount of clutter that sits on top of the desk. I then scan the area for the quantity of books piled up behind the desk, and then the flow of the overall space. Most often, if the circulation desk is clean and orderly, most everything follows suit. Books are put away, the space is pleasant and facilitates access, and the result is that the inhabitants look comfortable and peaceful as they are studying, or completely absorbed as they participate in activities. The librarian is typically well paced and helping people as they need it. Yes, when this is happening, as an observer of stakeholders within the space, I can stand there at length being virtually unnoticed. But it won't be long before the librarian acknowledges my presence. This is because they are organized, attentive, and welcoming to whomever walks through the door.

However, libraries with the appearance of disorganization tend to have patrons who fly back and forth from one area to another or wander about aimlessly. Groups of people seem to bounce into and off of each other. The librarian looks either overly energetic with a plastered smile on their face or on the verge of being frantic with a look of distress trying to keep up with the patrons. If the librarian has been operating like this for years, they look tired, worn, and somewhat defeated. When I enter the room, nobody notices me because they are consumed. It's exhausting!

I've been both of those librarians over the course of 20 years. At first, I was okay with the fast pace of high-energy chaos. It can *feel* exciting and productive. But if you're not feeling well, or you reach the end of the day, or you've operated like this for years, the atmosphere starts to work against you. You risk being swallowed up by unshelved books, incomplete paperwork, unweeded materials, and a messy environment. You either give in to the state of affairs or you work longer and harder to fix it all. But I eventually learned that I could take measures to ensure that I was operating in the version of a library that made me most comfortable. Having been a soloist librarian in a small school, a public librarian working with a small staff at a branch library, and then back to being a school librarian with an assistant but soon to be a soloist again, throughout these phases in my career, I've relied on either volunteers, staff, one assistant, or students. At times, I was the only one there to do all the work myself.

I learned that I could organize several key tasks so that dedicated volunteers or staff would be able to share in my responsibilities. With some simple space changes, then clearly defining tasks, processes, and responsibilities, I was able to be certain that whoever was hired or volunteered to help was truly able to contribute, and this afforded more time to plan for quality library programming for students or the public to enjoy.

But when there are no other employees or volunteers, it's even more essential to refine your plans or establish routines so you can become as efficient as possible. By taking time to make your processes "lean," you can continue or begin to provide a quality library and programs while simultaneously accomplishing the responsibilities of managing a library and its holdings.

When budget cuts were widespread across the nation around the early 2010s, for many librarians, decreases in funds resulted in staff cuts. Not surprisingly, the expectations for library service from administrators or the public did not proportionally decrease. For self-preservation purposes, and to prove the point that more help was needed in the library, decisions were made by librarians everywhere.

One option for school librarians was to choose to focus either on managing a collection or on teaching, but neither would be performed at the same level as they had been before the decrease in staff. I heard this from librarians across the nation: "If you want me to teach, I'm not going to worry about the shelves." Or "I don't have time to teach when all I can do is get books checked out, checked in, and back where they belong!" Similarly, public libraries cut back on hours of service to adjust to decreases in staff. The result, in both cases, is that service suffers.

A second option was to determine to keep up the service, remain at work well after hours, attempting to complete all the tasks that didn't happen during the day. This is an excellent option until you have family business to attend to, or you get sick, or worse, burned out. At that point, catching up feels impossible, and the only person who suffers is you.

The third option is to continue as usual and walk out at the end of the day, no matter what was left undone. If you can live with piles of unshelved books, unfiled papers, unspent funds, and mounting unmet responsibilities, then no worries! But at some point, you will be forced to live a life of managing emergencies, missing deadlines, and being held accountable for not doing your job adequately. For me, none of these options were acceptable.

Disarray is debilitating and I couldn't give up on my need to continually improve on the craft of teaching in the library. Giving up on order in the space and on my need to be a lifelong learner would have made me miserable, and it just doesn't make sense that a customer service person, such as a librarian, should continue on, feeling resentful and bitter, in a career that is so undeniably customer service oriented. Facing these options with their accompanying dilemmas leads me to tell you about my two, very dear friends.

Greg and Janice Gonzales have been my husband's and my friends for over 20 years. Our children are the same ages, they attended the same schools, and we are remarkably similar in our goals, values, and outlook on life. Because of this, we get together from time to time to have dinner, laughs, and catch up on our lives in general. At times, we also lean on each other when things aren't going quite so well. One evening, I needed to talk about how difficult it had become at work after losing my instructional assistant due to budget cuts. Trying to teach, manage the classes, books, budget, and my time were making work very stressful for me. My conversation was directed to Janice, whose profession is social work. She is an exceptionally good listener. But Greg stopped his conversation with Robert, looked at me with a combination of confusion and surprise, and said, "Elizabeth! Why didn't you tell me this sooner? It's what I do for a living!" I knew Greg worked for a certain multinational company that specializes in logistics and delivery. But his exact function as an industrial engineer was somewhat of an enigma to me. Greg proceeded to explain how one aspect of his job is to visit companies to study their operations and warehouses, make recommendations that lead to efficient operations, and those efficiencies lead to saving employees effort and time. The result is that employees are more productive and safer, and accordingly, the company increases customer satisfaction, and the final outcome is that it becomes more profitable. Greg decided at that very moment that he would take a day off from work to observe me in the library. He would make recommendations, and I, too, could become more efficient and safer and able to perform all of the duties that were expected of me, while saving me from burnout.

However, the day before our appointment, I called Greg to cancel. Despite his being one of my very best friends, with only my best interests at heart, I felt strangely nervous about being scrutinized for how I did my work and being observed for efficiency by an industrial engineer. Greg said that this was a natural reaction and reassured me that all he would do is follow behind me as I went about my usual business collecting books, checking them in, sorting them, and putting them on the shelves. The following morning in the library, it didn't take him long before he finished noting my activities, looking at the space, and finalizing notes. He smiled at me and said, "I've seen enough. I'm going home to write up some recommendations for you."

With those recommendations, and further instructions for me to go and learn about process management, Greg was able to help me find new life and enthusiasm for my job! After changing what used to be an exhausting, never-completed task of managing—what he described the library as essentially—a warehouse of books to an extremely manageable and highly functioning space, I now had time to continue with my love of self-improvement in the instruction of students. I also developed a passion for refining my tasks at work and making the space even more accommodating to meet all my and my students' needs. With the newfound time, I was able to go home at reasonable hours with my work completed for the day, feeling whole, and able to do other things at home. I was able to contemplate ways to provide my students with blended learning opportunities. With my newfound time and energy, I developed innovative ways to manage a whole school research program in the library setting. With a librarian-led, school-wide Genius Hour program that I conducted in an efficient and productive manner, my students and I thrived on the excitement of self-selected research, or passion projects. And the arrangement I had made of the space and the way I operated the daily routines within the library served everyone in meeting those goals.

Since then, I have accepted an administrative position in my school district. In this position, one of my privileges is to visit campus librarians and support them in meeting their needs and goals. When I visit these campuses, I see that many are still struggling with the day-to-day maintenance of the library as I once did. Even when I visit other libraries, such as small and rural public libraries, I can see areas for improvement to the organization of desks and space. There are simple changes that make a difference in the ability to increase service and decrease effort spent on tasks. Even larger libraries that are already well run still have areas for improvement.

However, I have also learned that when suggesting measures for improvement to an unsuspecting individual, the initial reaction is an insistence that the environment established there is precisely as it needs to be to get the job done. A messy desk "has everything where I can find it." The pencil holder stuffed with an abundance of broken-tipped pencils and dry-inked pens is there "because I like it that way." Keeping popular materials in the back of the library and less circulated items in the front? "It works for us!" Their routine is their routine and never has it been questioned before, so obviously it's okay! Understandably enough, the use of library space can be personal because it is a direct reflection of the people who manage it. Nobody wants to be told that they are living in a mess that they've caused and are in urgent need of help.

So, if you feel a sense of anger or fear welling up inside of you at the thought of moving even just one paper clip to a different location, that moving any one of these chairs would result in impending doom, that straightening up will ruin your life, put this book down and move along. There is nothing for you to see here! But if you can leave all of your fears and insecurities aside and take some time for deeper reflection, you may now be a little more open-minded—at liberty—to think that maybe you could do yourself a favor and consider the notion that change can be good. Maybe you can take some time to come to the realization that you just don't want to deal with the library the way it is anymore—especially if you don't have to. If you know that you have better things to do than to waste your precious time with unnecessary actions to accomplish what should be a simple task, if the library that you manage seems to be working against you instead of for you, then read on! When you have decided that your own personal well-being is far more important than proving a point to administration that more staff should be hired, that you are ready to provide the solid library service that you were trained and are qualified to provide, then this is the book for you!

Remember, when you begin, that you will be working to fix things for yourself—*only* for yourself. Positive change begins when you start by learning how you can manage the library space and the activities that you need to happen within it. You will reap the benefits that come when you apply key concepts from other industry practices to all aspects of libraries, not just the shelves. You will decrease the amount of time you spend getting routine tasks accomplished when you discover the fundamentals of industrial engineering and process management, sparing you the outrageous math that the professionals use to get there! You will examine the essential health and safety recommendations as they apply to library tasks, and routines to help you protect yourself from injury and increase the odds of a long and healthy career for you and anyone who works alongside of you. You will also be introduced to basic fund and cost accounting principles that will help manage your budget and establish solid record-keeping practices. And finally, you will gain a basic knowledge of vocabulary and information from architecture and design that will help you participate in the decision-making process for changes in existing or new construction of library space if the opportunity presents itself.

It is my hope that you will enjoy this book by taking your time reading and implementing one simple task at a time, over an extended period of time. By gradually adapting to each of the 10 things to improve your library space in a deliberate manner, you can see improvements in your ability to provide better service and you'll enjoy your profession more. I also hope that after you have gained that experience, you too will have a problem! You'll now know how to continuously make improvements to your activities and experience all the benefits of being more efficient and in control of your space and how you improve library service.

Here's to you, lifelong learner. Enjoy the process!

# PART 1

# Creating an Efficient Library

CHAPTER ONE

# Regain Your Evenings and Weekends

Americans have a reputation for working far too much. A Gallup Poll in 2018 reported that 44 percent of both full- *and* part-time workers work more than 44 hours per week. A 2014 Gallup Poll, reporting the work habits of only full-time workers, indicated that the majority of salaried employees claimed to work up to 47 hours per week. With almost one full day of *non-compensated* work per 40-hour workweek, along with habitually eating at a desk while working, answering e-mails at home, not taking allowed vacation time, family leave, or breaks, this begs the question, "Why are people doing this to themselves?"

According to the State Library Administrative Agencies (SLAA), the funding of state library services has decreased over the past 12 years by 22 percent. The result of reduced budgets has led to decreases not only in expenditures for resources, but also in staff and service that is provided (Peet, 2018). Similar circumstances have occurred in schools and public libraries. Cutbacks at the state and local government level have led to decreased numbers of employees that work in schools and public service agencies. Unfortunately, instead of the workload proportionately decreasing, the remaining employees are now left with all the tasks and responsibilities that are required to continue the same level of library service as it would have if it were fully staffed.

If fewer employees, or you alone as a soloist, must fulfill the responsibilities of a purchaser, manager, reference librarian, circulation attendant, as well as the children's, young adult, and adult's librarian, then managing to successfully perform all these tasks can be exceptionally challenging. Forging through tasks as quickly as possible can lead to mistakes that can be costly, or taking adequate amounts of time to get a job done properly can result in a long list of unaccomplished tasks at the end of the day. Either way, it forces conscientious workers to feel the need to work nonstop all day and long past regular work schedules. Working without breaks or vacation still won't yield enough time to complete all the tasks. Furthermore, the lack of rest can have the exact opposite result of what someone hopes to accomplish. Instead of getting it all done, the effect of relentlessly managing an unwieldy workload leads to ineffectiveness, which manifests in stress and results in burnout, illness, or injury.

Dr. Alice Boyes, in an article published in *Psychology Today* (2018), stated that "Sometimes working long hours can lead to being ineffective, especially if you keep grinding away when what you really need to do is mentally step back and get perspective on what you're doing." In addition to the stress caused by task overload, there are other situational factors that can have the same result. When you are called to serve the public as a librarian, you have most likely taken the job because of your desire to help people, coupled with your love of being a lifelong learner and disseminator of information. But at times, the people to whom you have availed yourself can bring complications to your day. Everyone, at one time or another, has found themselves working with less than agreeable people, be they patrons, bosses, coworkers, or volunteers. It can be unnerving not knowing when someone might become unusually upset about how difficult it is for them to locate materials, or what the reaction will be when finding materials that they perceive to be offensive, or how they will handle the news when they discover they have lost or overdue fines. It is also frustrating when people take it upon themselves to move heavy furniture or large numbers of materials to suit their needs and fail to return them to their original location. Likewise, a difficult boss may foil your ability to accomplish *your* responsibilities, especially when the boss is not organized or able to provide you with enough notice to meet deadlines within a reasonable amount of time. Coworkers or volunteers may not be as productive or cooperative as you need them to be, and when the undone tasks fall on you at the end of the day, your evening departure will be delayed or your morning to-do list will grow to unmanageable numbers of tasks that cannot be accomplished in a limited amount of time. When any or all these factors come into play, the result is stress. This causes you to be distracted, it makes you vulnerable to illness or injury, and subjects you to extended work hours.

If you acknowledge that there are forces in play over which you have little to no control, you can also recognize that there are tasks over which you do have varying degrees of control. Completing paperwork; answering e-mails; placing orders for materials; planning and preparing library programs, lessons, or special events require only the librarian's time and attention when alone or uninterrupted. Processing materials, checking in and shelving books, and cleaning up after patrons are tasks that require time, but those can only be accomplished after the tasks are initiated by library users. Reference questions or instruction or assistance to patrons who need help locating materials are processes between two people that cease once the information needs have been met. All these events, with the help of process management techniques, can be accomplished in a manner that takes the least amount of time and ultimately makes the tasks effective and pleasant for all involved.

When you have learned to target and improve tasks, you may even notice that the way the library is configured may also be slowing you down. Reconfiguring library space can be within your control! Simply relocating the place where tasks are most easily executed or where books can most effectively be discovered can have dramatic effects on the amount of time you spend in collection management–related activities.

Once you gain awareness of obstacles or hindrances, analyze them. Determine if these tasks are within your control to improve them, and acknowledge that you don't need to accept the status quo. If you realize that you have the ability to change the existing state of affairs, you would probably also agree that working all day without stopping, staying late, or arriving early to barely keep up with all-consuming duties at work every day is unacceptable. Taking incomplete tasks home to catch up is not a satisfactory remedy for you or your family, either. Maybe now you would also agree that if there are better ways to perform your daily tasks—not so that you are operating like a machine, but that you are operating in a way that makes you more human—then investing some time now in order to change things for the better in your very near future will be time well spent. If you can envision what a better work environment could be for yourself, it would be worth the effort to bring that vision to life. If someone could give you some practical steps that you could take here and now, you would be highly motivated to take those steps to create a happier workplace for yourself, volunteers, or coworkers. All you would need to do is make sure that you, and everyone who participates in your community's library, are able to acquire the skills necessary to make these changes in some key tasks and space that help make this a reality.

When you are ready to make changes to improve your existing circumstances, you will see that by identifying and improving factors *within* your control, you will also become better able to handle the factors that are *outside* of your control. When you evaluate the time and the place that you work on certain tasks, you can begin to evaluate whether your time was spent wisely or whether the space facilitates the task. When you can pick certain tasks as candidates for improvement and begin to make modifications to improve it, you will instinctively know that the task has taken far too much of your time because of extraneous distractions or obstacles that prevent you from working in a satisfactory manner. When you develop an eye for identifying problems and finding solutions, you will be primed to make the changes that will give you time to do the things that are truly meaningful to you, like fulfilling your desire to help people; spending time in pursuit of being a lifelong learner and disseminator of information; and, yes! You may even be regaining your evenings and weekends.

### Case Study

An elementary librarian in her second year of service works at a campus of approximately 650 students. As if a new career isn't stressful enough, she also has the added responsibilities of a toddler child, a sick father, a husband who is preparing to return to school, along with meeting the ongoing demands in education.

She is not a stranger to hard work. "Working and going through school for [my master's degree] took a lot of time. I had the baby when I started school, worked all day as a teacher, and then came home to help. I would stay up until midnight getting my work done.

"My husband had to be a single parent. He was an incredible support. He is a nuclear medicine technologist and wants to get CT certification too, but he put his education and training on hold for me. Now, next year, he's ready to start his program and I'm hoping to save more time so I can return the favor."

This librarian is highly motivated to do her job well, to successfully collaborate and be a leader on her campus, and to help her family successfully meet their goals now and in the future. "We grew up poor, and we want to do everything we can for stability, and a better quality of life for us and our child."

As a classroom teacher for 12 years, she tried to be as efficient as possible. "My first principal wanted her people to get out by 4:00. She was big on work life and home life balance. I didn't want to bring work home and I didn't want to spend hours after school, so I looked for ways to get things done with my teaching partner so as not to do more work than necessary. I didn't want to work against myself."

In her first year of librarianship, this librarian had seen a webinar that I presented on library efficiency and then recently found the summary of this book in the ABC-CLIO catalog. She began a conversation with me by saying that she "really needs this book!" She continued by explaining that she likes efficiency. "I don't like to do the same thing over and over, doing it in a time-wasting way." In the webinar, I offered a few simple techniques to expedite the process of checking in and shelving books. "Staging books helps me return the books to the shelves quickly." From this book, she wants to learn the things that she wouldn't have thought to do on her own. "Ten things sounds manageable. And I'm ready to do whatever I can to help make my work life better."

With her newfound time, she plans to spend time with family and be able to read books, "not just listen to audio books!" (Which I thought was an excellent way to catch up on books while doing other things like exercising!) Professionally, however, she needs more time to prep for lessons, write lesson plans, and work on her library budget. "Last year, I didn't need to make lesson plans, but now the [whole faculty has been asked to adopt a uniform plan] and it's taking time for everyone to make it work with their usual lesson plans, and I also need more time for that. And working on the budget? That is ridiculous!"

"Sometimes people are offended when you tell them that the routine they've used for years may not be the most efficient. Do you feel that way?" I asked.

"Oh, no!" she answered enthusiastically. "I'm new to the library, and I believe there is no reason to reinvent the wheel. [Before I was in education,] I was a waitress. And waitressing was tough. You have to find the best, most efficient way to do things. [Because] I would have to go to different stations to get what customers needed, I learned to get the answers to all the questions [about selection] so I could get everything they needed at once. My mother worked in restaurants, and I learned it from her. My mom would say, 'Don't be lazy. Do it right the first time and save yourself some effort.'"

Knowing that there may be a better way—being open to suggestions and being determined to work smarter, not harder—will help this librarian accomplish her personal and professional goals. She, like so many others, has a great number of responsibilities both inside and outside of the library, but taking a bit of time now to make your tasks easier in the future is only the first step in building the kind of work and home life that you want for a happier life.

## References

Abadi, Mark. "6 American Work Habits People in Other Countries Think Are Ridiculous." *The Independent*, Nov. 17, 2017. www.independent.co.uk/news/business/american-work-habits-us-countries-job-styles-hours-hoilday-a8060616.html

Boyes, Alice. "Work Long Hours? How to Survive and Thrive." *Psychology Today*, Mar. 8, 2018. https://www.psychologytoday.com/us/blog/in-practice/201803/work-long-hours-how-survive-and-thrive

Gallup Inc. "The '40-Hour' Workweek Is Actually Longer—by Seven Hours." Gallup.com, Aug. 29, 2014. news.gallup.com/poll/175286/hour-workweek-actually-longer-seven-hours.aspx

Gallup Inc. "Work and Workplace." Gallup.com, July, 2019. news.gallup.com/poll/1720/work-work-place.aspx

Maatta, Stephanie. "Jobs & Pay Take a Hit." *Library Journal*, vol. 134, no. 17, Oct. 15, 2009, pp. 21–29.

Miller, G. E. "The U.S. Is the Most Overworked Developed Nation in the World." 20somethingfinance.com, Jan. 13, 2020. 20somethingfinance.com/american-hours-worked-productivity-vacation/

Moodie, Alison. "Why Are Americans Spending Too Much Time at Work?" *The Guardian*, June 30, 2016. www.theguardian.com/sustainable-business/2016/jun/30/america-working-hours-minimum-wage-overworked

Peet, Lisa. "IMLS Report: State Library Funding Still Suffering." *Library Journal*, vol. 143, no. 3, Feb. 15, 2018, pp. 10–12.

"Trouble at the Census Bureau." *Congressional Digest*, vol. 97, no. 2, Feb. 2018, p. 31.

CHAPTER TWO

# How to Become the Best Evaluator of What You Do

There is a story, or maybe it is just a joke, about a parent teaching a child how to make a pot roast. The instructions included a strict rule about cutting off both ends of the roast before placing it in the pan. When the child questions why cutting the ends off was necessary, the parent says, "That's how Grandma always does it." The child, not accepting whether this would improve the outcome of the meal, calls Grandma to find out what precisely was the reason for cutting the ends off of the meat. When Grandma answers the question, she states, "It's so the pot roast will fit in my pan." Some people firmly believe that they are doing everything precisely as they should be done because there isn't any other way—without a real understanding of the purpose.

If you adhere to a certain routine for no evident reason, maybe now is the time to question why you do the things you do. Solid librarianship standards promote the practice of teaching others how to be lifelong learners. To do this effectively, the librarian must be a lifelong learner, too. When you feel the need to improve; when you can question the purpose or logic of the way, or the *why*, you perform certain tasks; when you feel that your efforts are not as effective as you would like them to be, you increase your ability to become an evaluator of your own work and how you perform your duties. With some objective processes and approaches to create a real plan of action, and methods of executing steps in a logical way, you will be able to develop a critical eye for improving or refining your work and space.

## A Self-Prescribed Growth Plan

Anyone who receives an annual evaluation that is based on a "growth plan," knows it can be infuriating when you are told that there is so much more room for improvement, especially when you have gone above and beyond the call of duty or you are doing everything in your power to perform at your absolute best. But working harder, faster, longer, or stronger will wear you out over time, and it will go unnoticed or unappreciated when you are unable to surpass that level of performance year after year. So, for the sake of helping yourself to save time now and in the future, try to dismiss the negative feelings that are stirred within your soul when the words "growth" and "plan" are spoken together, and consider how redirecting your intentions and actions toward embracing a "growth plan" that you initiate yourself, for yourself, can help you to protect yourself from burnout or physical injury by working smarter.

Your personally created, professional growth plan will begin when you can think like this:

> *I will embrace the mindset that I am the best evaluator of the processes that I employ, as well as the space that I utilize, to perform my work.*

When you welcome the idea that there is always room for "growth," that there are clear, objective actions to be taken to improve the circumstances that cause you to feel tired, frustrated, or defeated, you will be on your way to becoming the best evaluator of what you do. You cannot be judged negatively, and you will not reprimand yourself. Any changes you seek to make come from your desire to make your circumstances better, not more burdensome or unrealistically demanding. By being your own most compassionate, constructive critic with an objective and deliberate, actionable plan, you can learn how to embrace the things that you already do well and adjust the things that need improvement.

## Introducing Process Management

Process management, according to the Business Dictionary, is defined as administrative activities used to define a process or tasks and to identify opportunities for improvement (Business Dictionary, 2018). According to James Riley, author of *Process Management*, there are three principal dimensions for measuring how well you are executing certain tasks. These dimensions are effectiveness, efficiency, and adaptability.

You will know that the processes you are engaged in are *effective* if the results are meeting your or your library users' needs. For example, effectively maintaining patron accounts means that you have taken measures to make sure that the library management system, or circulation program, accurately reflects the number of materials currently checked out. It could also mean that the patron's account accurately reflects fines or fees accumulated. In the most essential of tasks, the list of items checked out on a patron's account is decreased by the number of books returned or increased by the number of items checked out by scanning the bar code. Effective management of patron accounts could also mean e-mailing notices to patrons before books become overdue to avoid the discomfort or inconvenience of assessing overdue fees. Another example of effectively managing patron-related processes is returning books or materials to the location where they belong quickly and accurately so the items can be easily located again.

"A process is *efficient* when it is effective at the least cost" (Riley, 1999). If reference questions can be answered and the necessary resources are available to answer the question, then there has been efficient acquisition and use of a librarian's time and the library's materials. In a library, costs can be expressed in terms of time. If opening a library in the morning can be done quickly, with the least amount of effort, the opening routine is efficient. If a patron can locate materials quickly and independently, the library is organized efficiently.

The processes that you execute in the library are considered *adaptable* when they remain "effective and efficient in the face of the many changes that occur over time" (Riley, 1999). In the library, the space and organization need to be adaptable because patrons' need for certain types of materials or service will be different over the course of time. Typically, patron needs and reference questions change as the types of materials and technologies change. If libraries are to be adaptable, the library space should be reconfigurable, and the librarian must be willing to learn and grow professionally, in response to innovation and technology.

---

### CASE STUDY

A librarian was confronted by her supervisor about the lack of accessible tables in the library. The supervisor wanted to be able to have meetings without scheduling them ahead of time, and the demand for immediate availability made it stressful for the librarian. Because office space and storage were cluttered and unavailable, the library tables were often occupied with projects that were in progress. This situation made both the supervisor and the librarian unhappy.

The demands on the library, for both usable gathering space and a makerspace, were necessitating a change in the arrangement of shelves, storage, and workspace. To do this, we began by clearing out storage space that was permanently holding obsolete equipment and technologies that were in disrepair. We weeded excessive and unmanageable numbers of books waiting for repairs and relocated games and maker kits to shelves behind the circulation desk so they would be accessible to the patrons but away from the tables where meetings would occur. A nearby break room that was being used as storage was repurposed as a makerspace room. All the clutter that was taking up space was either removed from the library or placed where it belonged. Rooms and storage that were now clutter free became working spaces or places to hold and make more accessible the valuable, usable equipment and supplies that both the librarian and the patrons needed. Now the larger space in the library was freed for meetings and events at a moment's notice.

Before she took on this "organization project," the librarian recalls, "the stress was making me unhealthy, and not feeling well was not a doable situation for me. I was staying late every day—until seven or eight o'clock every night." She also stated that even with staying late frequently, she "couldn't get unburied."

She believes that there was a "kind of organization" created by the predecessor librarian, "but it wasn't *my* organization, and I think I needed to have ownership over the process. I think it is good to go through the space and decide whether or not [what is already there] works for you."

When I asked her what is different now since we cleaned up and reorganized, she stated that she changed her priority to not staying late. "One late night is all I do. But I have to do this for me because undone [tasks] wake me up at night or bother me into the evening. It is worth it to stay once or twice a week to get back to save your well-being. But I make sure I meet my goal to be home at a certain time."

Staying late on a weekly basis may still be too much, so I asked what are the causes of falling behind? "I have big clubs that keep growing and an abundance of donations to deal with. I get new things that don't have a home, and I need to find places for them." When you visit this library, customer service is the priority as the librarian always stops what she is doing to address the patrons' needs and concerns. Her programs are well attended. However, in addition to finding space for lots of donations, she also spends a great deal of time on collection development. She painstakingly analyzes each book for number of circs, decides whether a replacement needs to be acquired, scrutinizes the vendors for better bindings and better customer service. As she tells me all the steps that she takes to weed and purchase new books, I think to myself, "We can work on that."

Maintaining an organized space requires relentless action, effort, time, and practice, especially to achieve it in small increments instead of regularly taking large blocks of time to keep things under control. Efficiency in this area doesn't magically happen overnight.

I ask if things stay organized all the time. "Oh, no!" the librarian answered. "Blowups happen, but the organization guts are still there. With the changes in the storage area, before there was no place to put things, but now I'm able to send a helper to go [into the storage room] and put things back where they belong. I make sure my makerspace shelves are organized and ready for more projects. Sometimes, things slip away in places, but [I realize that it is] not as bad as it looks. I remind myself that this goes back here . . . and that goes there. And I can get it all put away in less than fifteen minutes because the core underpinnings are there."

I wonder, based on her report of the weekly late work nights, if she is satisfied with the organization of the library. "Would it be a bad thing for [you to come back for a] revisit? No." she says honestly. "It wouldn't be such a bad thing to take a deep breath and take some time to look at what is working and what isn't working. It's tough to manage time to clean up on a regular basis. But something I've learned to do is to have things on carts. By keeping the things, I need to work on mobile, especially since I don't have a lot of counter space, I can put the cart away when I don't have time to work."

And what about the supervisor and the pop-up meetings? Is she able to clear things out quickly?

"Absolutely!" She said.

## Where to Begin

If you have decided that you accept the challenge of a self-created "growth plan," to become effective, efficient, and adaptable, by making a conscious effort toward improving service for your patrons to meet their needs, as well as your own, the question is, where do you begin? As a soloist librarian, or as a member of the team, it is a good idea to begin with the processes and spaces for which you are solely responsible before you move on to tasks that will require others to learn or share in a process and adapt to change.

Beginning with tasks that affect only your responsibilities will give you experience on a small scale. Then once you have some experience with managing your space and processes, you can work your way to spaces and routines that directly impact others. If you begin at the beginning, being patient with yourself, taking time while implementing 10 simple changes, you will be well on your way to saving yourself time and improving service to your patrons.

The 10 changes you can make are these:

1. Organizing your desk
2. Analyzing your daily routines
3. Creating routines for purchasing and receiving
4. Creating a receiving, processing, repair station
5. Implementing procedures for effective communication
6. Managing storage and reordering of supplies
7. Analyzing causes of stressors and taking precautions
8. Weeding and clearing the library space
9. Reconfiguring the library space
10. Preparing for refurnishing, renovating, remodeling, or new construction

As you take on your "self-directed growth plan" and focus on the processes that must be performed in the library, the result will be that you will effectively be meeting your and, equally importantly, your patrons' needs. As with all process management improvements, the goal is to yield improved customer satisfaction—even though you are beginning by improving what you do and how you do it for yourself. When you improve your own space and tasks, and then the space and tasks that directly impact your patrons, you will be increasing time and opportunities to provide improved customer service, thereby increasing the odds that the library is perceived as an indispensable part of your community, and worthy of future investment.

## References

Gardner, Robert A. "10 Process Improvement Lessons for Leaders." *Quality Progress*, vol. 35, no. 11, 2002, pp. 56–61.

"Process management." Definition. BusinessDictionary.com, www.businessdictionary.com/definition/process-management.html.

Riley, James F., and J. M. Juran. *Process Management*. McGraw-Hill, 1999.

CHAPTER THREE

# Addressing Fears and Misconceptions of What Efficiency Will Bring

When staff has been eliminated due to budget cuts, it's normal for whoever remains to be expected to assume those responsibilities. It certainly feels like there is no benefit or justice for the remaining person to be responsible for all the work of two people and then do everything possible to fill the two roles. It feels like you are sabotaging your own well-being. Even when outsiders insist that after a round of cutbacks, if you still have a job, you should be thankful for surviving the layoffs. They try to console you with the statement, "You could be looking for another job." But that rationale doesn't address the fact that there are responsibilities that a missing staff member will not be there to perform. By stepping up, remaining staff wonder, "If I do all the work, don't I just prove to the school board, the city council, the commissioners court, the legislature that they were right to eliminate that position in the first place?" And what if one day the budget could be restored? Wouldn't it just ensure that additional librarians or staff would never come back if during lean times the two jobs were managed well enough by one person? Will this just give more evidence that the eliminated position was never necessary to begin with? The dilemma is very real.

There are some tasks that are more prone to postponement or omission than others: Collection management, programming and instruction, and professional development can be delayed for a very short period, but over time the negative results are exponential. Collection management, which includes weeding and returning materials to shelves, is something that requires continuous attention, and at times a wholesale, committed effort. Weeding a collection could be done between or during tasks such as removing damaged or worn books during check-in or when shelving to a limited extent, but to really work on improving the overall condition and relevance of a collection takes large amounts of time. Because of this, coupled with the fact that there is nobody urgently demanding that you weed, it is easy for a librarian pressed for time to say, "I'll take care of that later." The result, before you know it, is an aging collection that remains intact and becomes increasingly inaccurate or irrelevant. If new books are acquired, the shelves become stuffed to capacity and are difficult to negotiate. Shelving and searching become difficult for both librarian and patron, and the work that happens at the shelves requires an unnecessary amount of effort.

Returning materials to the proper location, another task associated with collection management, is one that may quickly make you feel is insurmountable if not attended to regularly. One problem with not returning materials on a continuous or regular basis is that you multiply the number of locations that need to be searched before the materials can be accessed. This applies not just to books that are returned after checkout, but also to newly purchased books that are not shelf ready, a shipment that remains boxed and unreceived, and to damaged books that have been removed from the shelves and placed in a different location for repairs.

When collection development and collection management are left undone, the worst outcome is inconvenience or wasted time. However, when library programming and instruction is sacrificed, the result can almost feel tragic. In a public library, even if you can "throw together" a quick story time session or project, perhaps your more affluent patrons will gain some benefit. But when there is little or no time for planning a cohesive, meaningful program, there is potential for lost opportunities to reach the underserved or at-risk patrons. There is a chance that you may fail to think of contingencies that will result in a failure to account for the needs of persons with disabilities. If you have sacrificed all other tasks in the library to make a great program happen, all your efforts might be wasted for the lack of adequate promotion of the event.

Furthermore, for school librarians, when there is only one person on staff, you risk being driven by merely circulating materials. Keeping up with the check-in, checkout, and replacement of materials back to the shelves may result in far less time available for planning lessons, collaborating with teachers, or preparing professional development for faculty. If the librarian resists the urge to make shelving a priority to be certain that well-developed, collaboratively planned lessons occur, the result may be a disorganized collection where the materials are not discoverable or easily accessible. When students and teachers are unable to enter a library and quickly find the materials that they need, they will spend all of their time searching and not enjoying the library and other activities. They will leave disappointed, at best. But very young students, who may not be able to understand that the book is temporarily "lost," may be reduced to tears when they are forced to leave empty-handed because the schedule demands that they leave. For older students, especially middle and high school–age students, when locating what they want or need is too complicated or fruitless, they will be far less likely to return to the library for materials or help in the future. Losing those students because of misplaced or displaced materials is a terrible outcome for not being organized with materials.

It is essential to remember that the children and young adults of today are the adults of the future. They will have formed an opinion based on their past experiences about the value of a library. The degree of helpfulness of the librarian, the number of resources that were available for their enjoyment or for academic success, the indispensable help or instruction that they received that made a difference in their lives—or lack thereof—all have the potential to impact the future of libraries. When a vote is to be made about where to spend tax dollars, these children who have now become voting citizens, or even legislators or administrators, will have only their past experiences on which to draw. They may even begin to question the purpose or value of a library. If the librarian has chosen to stand on a high ground based on the principle of not "picking up the slack," then collectively, we run the risk of providing evidence or reason to decrease or cease funding for libraries altogether.

One additional matter of great importance that may be sacrificed for lack of time is professional development. Not wanting to close the library so that children and adults go without the resources that they need is the reason most librarians cite when they fail to attend or seek out quality conferences, webinars, or self-study programs for their own professional growth and learning. Out of all the resources that the library has to offer, you must remember that you, librarian, are the most valuable resource of all. A knowledgeable instructor, provider of resources, and guide to all things informational takes time and effort to cultivate in yourself. Professional learning opportunities give you the ability to get recharged, to connect with people in your profession, and to be inspired by what they are doing in their communities. Professional development is your opportunity to remain a well-informed information specialist, current with leading-edge technologies, trends or changing demands, and ways to better serve your people. When you ignore professional learning opportunities, you do so to the detriment of not just yourself, but to the people you serve.

As you delay collection development, programming and instruction, and your own professional development, as time goes by it will become evident that these things must be completed if the library is to function properly. If you have other staff members, incomplete tasks on your part will cause an exponential multiplication of problems for everyone else. The effect of mounting omissions causes everyone to fall even further behind in collection and professional development, circulation, teaching and instruction, and basic service. Launching efforts to restore a state of order, or at least reach a somewhat manageable one, can be daunting.

But the reality is this: Whoever remains on staff, even if it is just you, will be held accountable.

When you are the only one present to face the reprimand of an unsympathetic boss, or to field the complaints of an irritated patron, explaining that you are only one person doing the work of two people will not be an acceptable excuse for very long. At some point, if you have given up and resigned yourself to living with the situation, or convinced yourself that you are okay with the state of the library, you will now also need to be prepared to continually defend yourself by reminding everyone that you have no help. Or you may decide that you are finished enduring these circumstances by opting for an early retirement or turning to a second career to find respite. But if neither of these scenarios are an option for you, you might begin to wonder if there is a way to reduce the stress somehow, so you can make your work life better so you can feel whole again. Job satisfaction is essential to good health, and if you have set your mind to improving your current situation, it is time to take action in your work environment for your own sake.

The reality is, unfortunately, that there will never be more hours in a day. Extending your workday to complete the duties of multiple people is fine occasionally, but not on a regular basis. If you increase your workday even just by one hour daily, you will find yourself exhausted, angry, and resentful. This is not a solution for someone, such as yourself, in a customer service–oriented, information profession.

Real solutions result from being restored to a level of operation that will improve customer service and restore you to a level of reasonable comfort. When you have taken measures to perform tasks that directly impact you, which indirectly affect your patrons, you will feel better able to handle your responsibilities, and you may even begin to feel that your tasks are manageable, and you may begin to enjoy your work again. You will be empowered to have more time to spend on the services that are visible and have direct impact on your community, such as lessons and library programs. What is generated when you provide quality programs or service is what businesses call "goodwill." **Goodwill** is an intangible asset that causes certain goods or services to be perceived as something of high value—it makes the business or service worth far more than the actual dollars that have been spent to build or provide it.

In the library, goodwill results from the feelings that your patrons experience when they receive the time and attention that they need from you—when they receive the assistance and expertise of a knowledgeable, professional librarian. Goodwill happens when you provide a program that launches a love of reading in children or a sense of awe and wonder in the learning process that then impacts student success in school. It is the pride or a sense of belonging in a library space that fills a need for gathering for working or learning either collaboratively or independently. And this feeling that your community experiences, the value that they hold because of the quality service that you've provided, is what makes a library indispensable. When you have successfully established goodwill in your community, it proves to legislators and administrators that the library is, in fact, worthy of funding.

Taking the 10 simple steps, and some time, to become more efficient so you can provide better service is essential so you do not waste your valuable time working against yourself. But if you fear that once you are able to manage all of the daily tasks by yourself you will then be assigned even more duties than you already had before, though it could be a possibility, it doesn't have to be the result. When you have already prepared yourself with answers to the question, "what are you, or will you be doing with your time?," you will be ready with an array of services that you can offer your community or spend more time providing so that you can improve library service for your community.

CHAPTER FOUR

# Wise Uses of Newfound Time

After implementing the 10 simple things, when you have managed to streamline your tasks and are now able to make it out of the door at a reasonable hour, you will need to be prepared with a good explanation of what you are doing when you are not overwhelmed with busywork when administrators ask, "What *are* you doing with your time?" You might fear that if you are not seen busily handling materials or buzzing around the entire floor of the library, you will have proven to administrators that they were justified in cutting positions. If you are not seen in a perpetual state of motion, you might worry that they will find more work for you to do or cut back on your hours because you have too much time on your hands. Both are possibilities if you don't have ready a list of the tasks that you are responsible for to articulate or demonstrate that you are performing.

The last thing you will want to do is create the perception that when you are done with routine tasks, there is nothing else to do. You are guaranteed to experience negative outcomes when your newly acquired time is spent on extraneous activities such as shopping online or talking on the phone to your significant other. You risk, if you are in a school environment, being pulled for other duties outside of the library and the space being usurped for other uses that the principal deems a priority over library service or programming. In a public library, library hours may be cut back, money could be diverted to other departments, or you may soon find yourself underemployed or unemployed when administrators evaluate whether the type of work that is being done could be accomplished with less experienced or unqualified staff. If you are new to librarianship, you may not be aware of all the tasks that need to be accomplished to do your job completely and well. Without immediate or firsthand knowledge of all these tasks, you may be caught off guard when a supervisor asks you if you are free to take up the slack for a missing faculty member or office staff.

To avoid being considered expendable, when you are freed from all of the repetitive "warehouse management" of the library, you need to be prepared to demonstrate that your expertise and skill set are providing the kind of services that led you to enter the library profession to begin with or that you need to spend time cultivating or acquiring these skills.

These activities include:

- Reference and instruction
- Collection development
- Acquisitions
- Cataloging
- Managing continuing resources
- Program planning and collaboration
- More efficiency

## Reference and Instruction

According to the American Library Association, "Reference librarians recommend, interpret, evaluate, and/or use information resources to help patrons with specific information needs."

Whether you provide reference assistance to people in the library, over the phone, by chat, or e-mail, you will need to spend time investing in professional development via webinars or conferences, getting acquainted with the collection, learning the content, and understanding special features of digital resources to better serve your community.

It is a good use of newfound time to browse the library shelves to determine where materials are located and what is inside of them. You can find free instruction in the help feature of digital resources, and vendors provide assistance over the phone or may be willing to sit with you in person to provide instruction. You might join a professional organization such as the American Library Association or your state library association, or participate in a librarians' LISTSERV. And if you serve a group of professionals in a special library, you may wish to join *their* professional organization to keep abreast of new developments in the industry so you can better serve your organization's needs. You will also want to explore resources that give you access to educational opportunities through your employer.

School and academic librarians need to spend time acquiring knowledge of resources so they can provide instruction to students and faculty on the use of materials, including digital resources. In addition to instructing students and providing staff development, a school librarian may also be responsible for providing technology support and instruction.

No matter what type of library you manage, you are there to either assist people individually or teach them in groups. Whether they come to you looking for suggestions for recreational reading or they are in dire need of resources to find answers to a problem, when you can draw upon your knowledge of resources such as books and databases, and help people find or teach them how to find the information that they need quickly, this can be an extremely satisfying part of librarianship. Especially when the people you are serving leave with exactly what they wanted.

## Collection Development and Management

Spending time studying the collection, analyzing it for currency, relevance, and accuracy, is imperative to make sure the information you provide to your patrons is authoritative and meaningful, useful, or entertaining. Making sure that materials are updated and weeded is also essential to prevent dissemination of misinformation.

All libraries require constant attention to the collection. Curriculum changes constantly, and a library in the school or academic environment needs materials that meet both students' and educators' needs. Special collections librarians need to be alert for changes in industry standards; look for trends and advances; and seek out the unique materials, websites, or databases that are vital to the work of the professionals they serve. For libraries that serve a religious group, social service organization, science research group, a technology-oriented school or business, a specific trade, form, or art, or historical society, it is vital to remain current in new developments while being cognizant of materials that have historically been of great importance or value to the clientele that the library is meant to serve.

For the general public, every day can bring new and diverse questions or changes. It is important to spend time observing or having conversations with patrons about their information or leisure reading needs. You can spend time studying circulation statistics, noting which materials are of greatest interest to the community. By doing so, you will be better prepared to respond to more common information needs and be able to acquire materials that will be of value to the people for whom the resources were purchased.

## Acquisitions

After determining content that is of greatest value to your stakeholders, it takes time and care to purchase materials that will improve the holdings for a library, especially when your budget is limited. Acquiring the best possible materials means seeking out and getting familiar with vendors and the types of materials they provide. Most large vendors offer access to an array of publishers' materials, but you may also wish to do business with smaller vendors that specialize in durable binding or foreign-language authentic text, which features materials written in a "language as it is actually used by native speakers communicating with other native speakers" (Lanford, 2014), or printed materials for people with visual impairment or dyslexia. Some publishers can be contacted directly for content for professionals in, for example, accounting or law. Once you have determined the company that you will or are allowed to negotiate with, you will want to make sure you that you are getting the best price possible with the best customer service and the best possible binding that you need. After completing paperwork and the order is placed, you will also need to be certain that you receive what you have ordered in full, and on a timely basis, before the invoice is paid.

## Cataloging

If you are a soloist librarian and do not have the support of a library technical services department, then you will be responsible for the cataloging or import of your MAchine Readable Cataloging (MARC) records to your library catalog. Whether you receive the records created by the vendor, copy catalog and edit, or create your own original MARC records, it takes concentration, time, and attention to provide an accurate description of the materials that are available in the library, and to be certain that those materials are easily discoverable within the catalog search. Cataloging can be a tedious and time-consuming task when done correctly. When it is not done correctly, resources can be wasted because the materials associated with the catalog record did not reveal the location of the item, does not properly describe the item, or the item does not appear in a search that a non-librarian user would naturally make. To be certain, time spent on cataloging library materials is essential for patrons to locate and access all the treasures that a library has to offer.

## Managing Continuing Resources

Providing newspapers, magazines, periodicals, journals in print, and serials takes time. First, one must acquire by placing an order. Second, regular receiving will take place either daily, monthly, bimonthly, or some other specified period. Third, organizing materials on a shelf or display, replacing old copies with the most current, and determining when back issues are no longer of value and should be removed from the library shelves are part of the regular task of managing continuing resources. Updating professional materials can be a time-consuming task because it requires attention to detail. Being the most current materials in print, regular, consistent maintenance of continuing resources is imperative.

## Program Planning and Collaboration

School and public librarians require time to prepare lessons and activities for their students or the public. Instructional or information sessions for children, young adults, or adults can be planned for delivery in the library either at a special event or on an ongoing basis. Community outreach helps to promote literacy to special groups that will benefit from the services of a library, outside of the library premises. Coordinating special programs with other departments or agencies is valuable for promoting things such as health and city services. Literacy programs such as book clubs, book festivals, or author visits are all exciting for the community and cause stakeholders to become invested in their library. The planning process requires that you make contact and contract with presenters, provide a venue, generate advertisement, coordinate volunteers, and acquire materials, supplies, or solicit donations to fund the event.

When you seek out experts or community leaders that you need to work with you to help bring quality library services to life, it takes time to build a rapport that will lead to a synergistic collaboration. In education, building trust with potential collaborators—the teachers—and informing them that you have certain skills to offer takes time and patience. Providing instruction to teachers on available resources such as databases and their features is essential so that teachers can utilize these resources with their students and both of you can increase the likelihood of student success. The teacher–librarian partnership is vital to schools and student achievement.

## More Efficiency

When you have been able to streamline tasks, routines, space, and your day, you will find that you are able to see even more activities to execute in an even more efficient way. Whether it is relocating materials to the point of need, rerouting a path of an activity, reworking a design, or fine-tuning a process, you may want to spend a portion of your newfound time becoming even more efficient, productive, serving others, or preparing for future tasks.

Whether or not you will need to justify what you do with the time that you have suddenly acquired, it is always a good idea to be familiar with other tasks that are ever-present and that you will likely need to perform. If you know someone will eventually be asking you what it is you do or need to do, or if you have some free time on your hands, memorize this list, and understand the essence of what these responsibilities mean and the amount of time it takes to do them well. It is best to be prepared ahead of time to explain and inform as eloquently and thoroughly as possible.

## References

ALCTS. "Acquisitions Section." Association for Library Collections & Technical Services. May 13, 2019. http://www.ala.org/alcts/mgrps/as

ALCTS. "Continuing Resources (CRS)." Association for Library Collections & Technical Services. Feb. 12, 2019. http://www.ala.org/alcts/mgrps/crs

ALCTS. "Cataloging and Metadata Management Section (CaMMS)." Association for Library Collections & Technical Services. Feb. 12, 2019. http://www.ala.org/alcts/mgrps/camms

American Library Association. "Become a Librarian." Education & Careers. Oct. 27, 2017. http://www.ala.org/educationcareers/libcareers/become

American Library Association. "Technical Services Librarian." Education & Careers. July 20, 2016. http://www.ala.org/educationcareers/libcareers/jobs/technical

"The Bunheads Are Dead." *American Libraries Magazine.* Nov. 9, 2009. https://americanlibrariesmagazine.org/2009/11/09/the-bunheads-are-dead/

Lansford, Lewis. "Authentic Materials in the Classroom: The Advantages." *World of Better Learning | Cambridge University Press,* Feb. 23, 2017, www.cambridge.org/elt/blog/2014/05/16/authentic-materials-classroom-advantages/.

"Librarians: Occupational Outlook Handbook." U.S. Bureau of Labor Statistics. https://www.bls.gov/ooh/education-training-and-library/librarians.htm

RUSA. "Professional Competencies for Reference and User Services Librarians." Reference & User Services Association. Nov. 16, 2017. http://www.ala.org/rusa/resources/guidelines/professional

# PART 2

# Ten Simple Changes

CHAPTER FIVE

# Change #1: Organize Your Desk

For some people, the concept of streamlining processes and space can be confusing or overwhelming when looking at an entire library as a whole. There are so many activities, designated spaces, and processes to conduct that selecting where to begin can be a challenge. Trying to start with the most complex of tasks or identifying the true source of a system failure might seem insurmountable. Targeting the wrong issues and a failed attempt at a big reorganization project may discourage you from making any further attempts to change processes again. However, as silly as this is about to sound, you can begin learning about process management and organization by starting with your desk. By beginning at your desk, you will experience a micro view of process management, gain practice and experience analyzing space and processes, and build the confidence that you need to take on even more challenging tasks. Examining your desk with new eyes will not only help you gain a better understanding of how process management can facilitate completion of more tasks in an efficient manner, it will help you to begin your efforts in a surreptitious way so you can learn at your own pace and self-evaluate without the judgment or the opinions of others!

### Gain a New Perspective of Your Desk

The first step in streamlining your desk is to stop thinking of it as a place where you "just do your job" or work at for eight hours a day. Even if you are rarely there, and your desk has become the handy, catch-all landing place to pile miscellaneous things that never seem to get put away, now is the time to reevaluate the value and purpose of your desk.

Everyone, including those who routinely spend more time on the floor or at the circulation desk, would benefit from having a clear, task-ready workspace that is exclusively your own. The reality is, even if you thrive on action or chaos, almost everyone has responsibilities that call for full, focused attention that cannot be achieved effectively in the middle of a public space or on a work surface that is full of clutter and distractions.

To place your desk into proper perspective, it's important to recognize that it is, in fact, a **process station**. Your desk is a place to perform a series of tasks or job assignments that are exclusively or primarily your responsibility. Viewing your desk in this way will help you begin to dissect the "what" and "how" of the daily routines or duties that you perform. Establishing in your mind that your desk is a space to facilitate the performance of your duties in the most efficient way possible, you will be able to take measures necessary to eliminate or reduce redundancy of actions, to effectively preserve or archive valuable information, and become better able to address more important things such as spending time serving patrons or collaborating with staff.

### Prepare an Action Plan for Your Desk

To begin to prepare an action plan for your desk, take some time to think about goals for yourself and the work you perform at your desk. You will need to:

1. Identify tasks that you perform at your desk.
2. Determine what tools, resources, or space you need to perform your job.
3. Prepare to clear the space so you can make the desk task ready.
4. Return to the desk only the items you need to accomplish your tasks.

### Identify the Tasks

To effectively begin an action plan for your desk, ask yourself the following questions: What are the tasks you are responsible for that require concentration, organization, or privacy? Are you responsible for expending funds; writing evaluations or incident reports; preparing lesson plans, presentations, or scheduling; or do you have conversations involving sensitive matters? Are you required to file hard copies of documents or archive them digitally? Do you regularly enter data, catalog, or process materials? Do you spend time working on new and creative lessons that are curriculum rich? Recall or spend a week or two taking notice of the tasks that you perform at your desk on a typical day. List the tasks on a piece of paper or a digital document.

After you have listed each of these tasks, begin to dissect each one by listing steps or routines or processes you perform to accomplish the entire task. Are there tools that you need to accomplish these tasks? Is there an order to the activities that will expedite the process? For example, when you check messages on the phone, should you write them down on a paper or immediately document issues or questions in a database or spreadsheet, keeping name, number, issue, in order of call received? You can then decide if it is best to handle the return calls immediately or perhaps wait until a later time after you have completed other tasks.

You can, by either recalling past experiences or taking time to note activities for a couple of weeks, determine if you are more successful at completing tasks by waiting for a certain time of day, or decide whether immediate action is necessary. For example, if you archive documents digitally, you could take time to determine if it is best to gather and scan each document immediately to ensure the preservation of important information, or wait for a certain time of the week so you can complete the process of scanning, destroying, or filing the hard copies all at once, in a routine and efficient manner. Is it better to plan your next lesson in the middle of your current round of lessons as you observe student response to the content, or do you feel that you are more successful after you have had time to assess student learning when your lessons are complete?

Considering, evaluating, and then reconsidering the steps and most efficient and effective execution of these tasks are all part of the cycle of process management. The next thing to consider are the tools, resources, and space that you'll need to complete your tasks.

### Tools, Resources, Space

For every task that you must perform, it is imperative that you have the tools, resources, and space to execute those tasks.

First, it is a time-saving matter to have the right tools, in good operating condition, available as you need them. Phones and headsets that operate properly so you can hear and be heard, computers that are reliable when they are turned on, printers or scanners for creating or archiving important documents, devices that are charged and ready for use—all of these may be necessary items that you would have located on or next to your desk so you can quickly complete your tasks. Also, if you regularly file hard copies of documents, a hole punch, stapler, and file cabinet should be nearby.

Next, resources of the right type, in sufficient quantities, are also needed to help you get your tasks completed. For example, one or two small notepads and a pen to jot down numbers or titles or author names will help facilitate a reference call when the caller needs help locating materials. However, if you have a pile of pens that includes those that work only some of the time, or pencils with broken leads, discard them immediately, and keep only the ones that are reliable every time you need it. If you are in the habit of writing down extensive information, consider keeping a larger notepad so you can accommodate your need to take more detailed notes. If you prefer to retain notes digitally, take the time to carefully select a note-keeping app or create a note folder in a cloud-based drive, and devise a digital filing system that will serve your needs for ease of use, accessibility, and portability. You may discover that having your notes in a digital format is more beneficial so that you can address them anywhere you go. As you plan your lessons, do you need a calendar to see how much time it will take to see a full rotation of classes? Do you need a curriculum guide or a scope and sequence to make sure you are covering curriculum in a timely manner? Do you need your computer, or pencil and paper, to write down your ideas to share with your teachers? For other resources such as staples, clips, or highlighters, make sure you prepare to gather the minimum number necessary to have on hand and that all are in working order. Anything more than the minimum number of items needed means you are converting your desk into a storage space, which doesn't help you complete your tasks.

Additionally, it is important that you have adequate desk space to complete your tasks. Nothing prevents efficiency better than lack of space and things falling off of a desk while one is working. Whether you are given a desk that is too small or very large but still cluttered with papers, personal effects, and an overabundance of supplies, you should make efforts to keep it lean and clean so you have sufficient desk space to work.

Determining whether there is adequate space on your desk includes determining whether there are tasks that you regularly engage in that require a large amount of space to complete, that are constantly in progress, or that might be shared easily with a volunteer or other staff member. If this is the case, a separate dedicated workstation is in order. One such workspace is most likely a processing station. Setting up dedicated spaces or workstations for a single task will be addressed in Chapter 8.

When people claim that the piles of mess on their desktops are really arranged so they know where everything is located, what they are really saying is they won't take the time to file papers, finish unaccomplished tasks, or put things back where they belong. What this can translate to,

Change #1: Organize Your Desk

from a business perspective, is unaddressed needs of customers, unpaid bills for creditors, or uncollected revenues from sales, which can lead to business failure. In libraries, the same haphazard approach can translate to loss of "goodwill" or damage to the perception that the library is an essential, productive institution that is worthy of an investment of limited funds. Furthermore, a desktop filing system that is known only to its owner is a recipe for gaps in service. No one would be able to step in and address incomplete tasks should you suddenly become unable, due to unforeseen circumstances, to perform your job. In the library setting, where the public is being served daily, this is an unacceptable outcome.

### Prepare to Make Your Desk Task Ready

Whether or not you are a fan of books and their authors such as *The Life-Changing Magic of Tidying Up* and *Spark Joy* by Marie Kondo, you cannot deny that minimalism and organization can provide a whole lifestyle change that makes streamlining and tidying a purposeful and lasting endeavor. But if you cannot commit to reading an entire book that asks that you anthropomorphize material things, you can still effectively apply Kondo's basic principles for organization to the process of organizing a desk at work.

You will begin by taking everything off your desk. With four file-sized boxes at the ready, you will examine and remove everything on the desk, beginning from the left-hand side of your desk, sweeping across the surface to the right.

As you examine the contents of the desktop, you should sort items into one of the following four categories:

- Books
- Papers
- Personal effects, and
- Everything else

Waste no time judging their value or worth. Treat each item in the following manner:

- All books should be put in the first box, which you have placed on the left-hand side of the desk surface.
- All papers, whether they appear to be important or not, can be placed in the second box next to the books.

- All personal items should be immediately placed in the third box, being careful not to damage breakables.
- Everything else, including electronics, tools, and supplies, should be placed in the fourth and remaining box.

Now that your desktop is clear, remove the boxes and take some time to dust it and wipe it with disinfectant! Clean your computer keyboard, as well. Not just to look fresh and clean; this step will help to improve your health and productivity. All the clutter that has been in the way has kept either you or your custodian from properly sanitizing that workspace. The result of the lack of cleaning, according to the Centers for Disease Control and Prevention, is that your desk and keyboard are most likely dirtier than the toilets in your building, which are cleaned regularly (CDC, 2007).

Now that you have a clean and beautiful surface, you can address the contents of the boxes.

## Books

For librarians, addressing the books should probably be the easiest of the categories to manage, so do this as a first step to experience immediate success. You should already have a clear understanding of the categories of books and their established locations. Books in good condition should be returned to the shelves with the rest of the collection. If they are new or damaged, they should be placed at a processing station so they can be prepared for circulation or repair. If you do not already have a processing station, designate a cart or truck for now, as your temporary processing station. Special collection materials, such as those reserved expressly for librarian use, can be placed on a shelf in your office or in a special collection space for professional resources. Damaged books should be weeded and boxed for removal. Any books that are from your own personal collection, that you do not need to complete your work, can remain in the file-sized box to take home where they belong. Taking books off of your desk places them in the best location so that they can be handled or accessed in the near future. Keeping them stored on your desk prevents them from being dealt with, utilized by another individual, or can hinder your ability to complete other tasks. An exception can be reference materials that you need to complete your work daily such as instruction or policy and procedure manuals, cataloging reference books, or user guides. However, many of these are available online for quick and easy reference, and if they are, take them away.

## Papers

Papers will require the most time and discernment. All of the boxed papers from your desk will be addressed soon after you have completed addressing personal items and everything else. Papers are either very important or trash, so you will need to be fresh and focused when addressing them.

Later, when you return to your desk that is clear and task ready, begin by separating papers into two groups: Group one is a pile of items that are in immediate need of attention, and group two includes items that should go directly to the shredder or the recycling bin. The items in need of attention are those that require filing or archiving such as paid invoices, packing slips, and completed contracts. They also include items that are open issues such as unresolved phone calls, incomplete contracts, or notes on work in progress. All of the group one items are what need to be addressed sooner rather than later. Group two items are anything related to tasks that are completed but not in need of retaining, such as notes that no longer make sense, junk mail, catalogs, and outdated periodicals. All of these can be either shredded first or directly recycled. If papers such as handwritten notes or single sheets of printed paper are not clearly recognizable as unimportant, err on the side of caution and shred them just in case they contain sensitive information.

Once all the unnecessary documents have been cleared from the desk, place the "to be addressed" pile in the middle of your desk in front of your chair either stacked neatly in a tray, on clipboards, or in a file folder, prioritized in order of most to least urgent. You can then complete each task on a clean and clear space.

## Personal Items

Personal items do nothing to help you perform tasks, they just make your space feel more comfortable or inviting to you. One to three decorative items of sentimental, not monetary, value can be strategically placed out of the way but still within sight, on your desk to personalize the space. A photo or object for a decorative touch, plus a beverage container for water or coffee, can remain if it doesn't jeopardize papers or equipment. Finally, whatever personal items that you need to be comfortable and focused at work, such as a sweater, hand lotion, or eyeglass cleaner, can be stored inside a desk drawer or a nearby cabinet until you need it. The goal is to keep the work surface clear and ready for action.

## Everything Else

Examine the box with "everything else." Having already determined the tasks that you ordinarily perform at your desk, you now know which tools and resources you need to return to the desk to help to accomplish these tasks. Return only the minimum number of items necessary. A power station on your desk is helpful for devices, phone, or tablet so they are charged and ready for use. Scissors, stapler, tape dispenser can be returned if necessary. One or two reliable pens, pencils, or highlighters will suffice. Any surplus or redundancy that remains in the box can be easily stored in a supply closet and retrieved later when needed. Being lean with these items will help you be more efficient because mess is out of your way.

Be aware that the initial organization of your desk for efficiency can take a couple of hours or more when doing it for the first time. You may wish to schedule an afternoon to accomplish this, or if necessary, do it before or after work hours. You will find that it is worth your investment of time now to eliminate time waste into the future. If it takes you longer than a couple of hours to accomplish, do not worry! Everything is already sorted and stored in boxes to be addressed at a later day or time. But be certain to keep the urgent document box or pile on your desk so you can work on it soon. The personal items and excess "other items" can remain under your desk in the boxes until you are able to continue the project. If you feel it is necessary, be sure to place a sheet of paper on the boxes with the words "DO NOT THROW" if there is a possibility that a custodian might mistake the boxes for garbage.

If several days pass and the boxes still remain under your desk untouched, because you just don't have time or you doubt whether or not you made the correct decisions, you may have just proven something to yourself. As long as you were able to complete your regular duties without the contents of the boxes, you can now be confident to rid the desk of these items once and for all.

After the initial desk organization project, you should now dedicate 5–10 minutes every day, at or near the end of the day, to straightening out your desk as part of your exit routine. Your exit routine will be discussed in greater detail in Part 2, Chapter 6. But know now, before you walk away from your desk for the final time of the day, you will ensure continued success if you place all books back where they belong, where they will be repaired, accessed, or used later; file important documents, throw away expired notes, or neatly stack papers to be addressed tomorrow; be certain your tools and supplies are where they belong or are replenished;

and place any newly acquired personal items in a bag to take home with you when you leave for the day.

## Just to Clarify, What Is *Your* Desk?

Before going through the process of organizing and streamlining your desk, maybe it is wise to clarify what exactly is *your* desk. In libraries, people often confuse public workspace for their own personal workspace, which can lead to problems, and therefore warrants this important discussion.

A personal desk is a work surface with a chair that is primarily or exclusively used by an individual, in a somewhat solitary manner, for no other tasks other than those that are assigned exclusively or primarily to that one individual. It is typically in a designated office space, whether enclosed by a wall or partition, or located in a remote part of the library in a back room or corner. In short, and far less formally, it's where you will perform the duties assigned to you that have an *indirect* effect on your patrons. These duties include purchasing materials or services, preparing reports, researching, working on presentations. It is where you complete paperwork, plan or prepare programming or lessons, return phone calls, or answer e-mails.

In contrast to the personal desk, there are other desks and workspaces that are undeniably *not* personal. The circulation desk, for example, is a workstation designated for tasks that you or a whole staff and the general public come together to transact. A circulation desk is therefore not a personal desk. Likewise, a processing station where multiple employees or volunteers go to prepare materials for circulation, and a materials receiving station where people open boxes, check packing slips, and verify the contents of the box are not personal desks.

Makerspace tables or workbenches that are located in a common area where the public will be studying, working, or creating cannot be considered personal desks. Likewise, the tables in a reading room are for the public. Both of these locations must be defined as *not personal* because decorating a vital public work, study, or creative space with someone's personal items conveys the message that the space is "claimed," and, objectively speaking, work is obstructed and efficiency hindered. Furthermore, a workspace where various individuals may share duties may be subjected to virus or illness due to the fact that personal effects keep the space from being properly sanitized on a regular basis.

Making the distinction between personal and nonpersonal workspace is, therefore, absolutely imperative, and personal items should be taken away from the circulation desk, shared processing stations, the shelves in the library, the tables in the reading room, and the makerspaces. All that should remain are the tools necessary to complete the tasks, and perhaps a container of hand sanitizer, in those spaces.

When you begin analyzing your own desk, you signal that you mean business! It's the first step in developing a critical eye for all spaces and processes throughout the library. When you make changes for yourself, you may be leading the charge for an office or staff. By demonstrating that you are willing to begin with your own most personal space, you inspire everyone who enters the library to be resourceful and efficient, and everyone will be glad to spend time dwelling in that space.

## References

Carver, Courtney. "How to Live in the Land of Enough—Space." Be More with Less, July 21, 2015. https://bemorewithless.com/how-to-live-in-the-land-of-enough-space/

Centers for Disease Control and Prevention (CDC). "Norovirus Outbreak in an Elementary School—District of Columbia, Feb. 2007." https://www.cdc.gov/mmwr/preview/mmwrhtml/mm5651a2.htm

Kondo, Marie. *Spark Joy: The Illustrated Guide to the Life-Changing Magic of Tidying Up*. Ten Speed Press, 2016.

Kondo, Marie, and Cathy Hirano. *The Life-Changing Magic of Tidying Up: The Japanese Art of Decluttering and Organizing*. Ten Speed Press, 2014.

Nicodemus, Ryan. "Start Here." The Minimalists. Nov. 14, 2018. https://www.theminimalists.com/start/

Pool, The. "Marie Kondo: How to Tidy Your Office Desk." YouTube, Jan. 20, 2016. https://www.youtube.com/watch?v=UElNicTxomo

CHAPTER SIX

# Change #2: Analyze Daily Routines

Do you remember the time that you were given, or gave, an assignment to write about how to make a peanut butter and jelly sandwich or do some other thing that seemed second nature? Well, that assignment was preparation for this very occasion. You could, quite simply, state that you need to get the jars of peanut butter and jelly and a loaf of bread and put it all together, but if you follow the directions literally, two jars and a loaf will sit alongside each other, not becoming a sandwich. If you take each of these ingredients and then step-by-step dissect the process of opening and placing, analyzing the tools needed such as the plate, a spoon, or a knife, and then consider the location of the items such as the pantry, the refrigerator, the kitchen counter, or a table, slowly the steps required to make a peanut butter and jelly sandwich come together and a sandwich is made. With the steps outlined, you can then get creative and save steps by rearranging them by location, eliminate steps by combining them, or if all else fails, choose to outsource by purchasing a ready-made sandwich if you lack the time or ability to make the sandwich yourself. Like the PB&J example, you will use similar techniques to streamline your library processes.

In this chapter, you will learn about how to begin using process management techniques to streamline daily routines such as:

1. Opening and closing the library
2. Gathering statistics

3. Conducting circulation, and
4. Shelving

Because all of these activities are universal to all libraries of all kinds, analyzing and streamlining these processes will help you to better serve your "customers," no matter how you refer to them: patrons, professors, parents, professionals, students, staff, or teachers. You will also see that when you conduct tasks in the library space as an efficient routine and organize your space to be efficient, you can spend less time involved in mundane tasks and more time focused on providing excellent customer service. An added benefit is that you may be able to go home at a reasonable hour and protect yourself from injury!

## Opening and Closing

For each day that a library is in operation, two events that happen without fail are the opening and closing of the library. The mere act of opening the door to patrons or finalizing activities at the end of the day is filled with a series of steps that must be completed successfully for the current or following day to run smoothly. It all begins from the moment you raise your keys to the front door in the morning and ends when you prepare to leave the library at the end of the day. But you may be skeptical, wondering how you could open and close a library in any other possible way? Chances are, there are time-saving measures that you can take to make your entry and exit easier.

Granted that a library is not a multimillion-dollar corporation, however, astute business leaders employ industrial engineers to reduce the number of steps to accomplish a task to create finely timed, precision operation. In a process, each step and action is scrutinized to eliminate interruptions, repetitions, or obstacles whenever and wherever possible. Because time means money, shaving off every possible second from as many tasks as possible means more work can be accomplished, which in turn increases profits! The goal for you in the library, however, is to simply save yourself from the extra steps and actions that serve no other purpose than to leave you exhausted at the end of the day. Not taking measures to streamline your daily routines may be preventing you from experiencing the true joy of your profession now or from being able to continue to perform your regular duties long into the future.

If you find it necessary to demonstrate or provide proof to yourself, your supervisor, or staff that there are processes that could be streamlined in

Change #2: Analyze Daily Routines    41

your library setting, examine this example of a simplified process analysis. Observe the details that you could look for in your library setting. With the analysis of your specific set of circumstances, you can begin to practice how to document current processes and how to streamline those processes to convince yourself, or others, that there is a better way. Taking the opportunity to learn how to analyze more processes, you will discover that it's worth spending a little time up front to save yourself lots of time in the future.

## A Practice Exercise

Just as you did when analyzing your desk, you can spend a short amount of time acquiring a critical eye for evaluating and improving routines in a way that may go unnoticed by anyone around you but will make a noticeable difference to you. By making objective observations of the steps you normally take before opening the library for service, you just might surprise yourself with how much backtracking, repeating, searching, or fumbling you do for a task as simple as getting the day started.

Take time one morning, when time permits, to try this. With a smartphone or other device with a voice memo feature, or with the help of a friend, note every step that you take just to get through the door and to your desk. Include in your notes the location where you are performing a task, every action you take to complete the task and mark the time when you begin to perform that task. Don't worry about documenting the time the task is completed because the following start time automatically marks the end time of the previous action. As you document your actions, remember that the more detail you provide, the more you'll be able to see steps that could be combined, rearranged, or eliminated. However, if you wish to begin simply, start with documenting the things that you do in a less detailed manner so you can at least get into the habit of making observations. Include any interruptions, if they occur. Do your best not to try moving faster than you normally would! This isn't a race. It is an exercise to determine which steps or actions are available for elimination, so you can start your day as a relaxed, communicative human being.

Table 6.1 is an example of the steps a librarian might take when entering a library in the morning. These are actual combined actions taken by two librarians. From the car to the door was one librarian at a branch of a public library, and from the front door to the office was a school librarian. The two sequences were joined for demonstration purposes.

**Table 6.1  Steps Taken in a Morning Routine**

List the actions you take from opening the library door to ending your personal routine before you begin with the floor. Then look for steps that can be consolidated or eliminated.

| Location | Steps | Time |
|---|---|---|
| Starts with: Exiting the car in parking lot | Turn car off. | 7:30 |
| | Finish listening to NPR program. | |
| | Remove KEYS from ignition. | |
| | Pick up lunch bag. | |
| | Pick up tote bag. | |
| | Pick up purse. | |
| | Open door. | |
| | Exit car. | |
| | Close door. | |
| | Lock door. | |
| | Place KEYS in purse. | |
| | Double-check car door is locked. | |
| | Locate cell phone. | |
| | Take KEYS out of purse. | |
| | Open car door. | |
| | Pick up cell phone off car seat. | |
| | Place cell phone in purse. | |
| | Lock car. | |
| | Place KEYS in purse. | |
| | Walk toward library front door. | |
| | Greet patrons waiting outside. | |
| At front door | Place lunch and tote on stoop. | 7:40 |
| | Take KEYS out of purse (taking some time to locate). | |
| | Place purse on stoop. | |
| | Unlock gate. | |
| | Unlock door. | |
| | Open door. | |
| | Turn around to gather purse. | |
| | Gather lunch bag. | |
| | Gather tote. | |
| | Enter library. | |
| | Close door. | |
| | Put KEYS in purse. | |

*(continued)*

*Change #2: Analyze Daily Routines*  43

**Table 6.1** (*continued*)

| Location | Steps | Time |
|---|---|---|
| At circulation desk | Walk to circulation desk. | 7:47 |
|  | Place lunch, tote bag, and purse on circulation desk. |  |
|  | Walk to the office door. |  |
|  | Take KEYS out of purse. |  |
|  | Unlock office door. |  |
| Office | Turn on office lights. | 7:49 |
|  | Answer ringing phone at office desk. |  |
|  | Complete call and hang up. |  |
|  | Walk to cabinet above the coffee maker. |  |
|  | Open cabinet. |  |
|  | Take out coffee filter and place on counter. |  |
|  | Take out creamer and place on counter. |  |
|  | Take out sugar and place on counter. |  |
|  | Close cabinet. |  |
|  | Walk to refrigerator. |  |
|  | Take out coffee. |  |
|  | Walk to coffee maker. |  |
|  | Put coffee filter in maker. |  |
|  | Put coffee in filter. |  |
|  | Take pot off coffee maker. |  |
|  | Walk to sink. |  |
|  | Fill pot with water. |  |
|  | Open coffee maker reservoir. |  |
|  | Pour water in coffee maker. |  |
|  | Close all coffee maker parts. |  |
|  | Start coffee. |  |
|  | Walk to circulation desk. |  |
|  | Get lunch, purse, tote. |  |
|  | Walk to desk. |  |
|  | Put purse and tote on desk. |  |
|  | Take lunch to refrigerator. |  |
| Ends with leaving the office to get floor ready |  | 8:15 |

Let's pause here for now. All the steps in the illustration above have very little to do with serving patrons but everything to do with getting yourself into the library and prepared. This entering, with interruptions and coffee preparation, took approximately 45 minutes. You might be thinking, "that's ridiculous, nobody does all that!" or "Oh, no! You aren't going to ask me to stop making my morning coffee!" But many people do go through a difficult process just to get through the door and settled to begin working. In fact, a back-and-forth, multistep route is not an uncommon part of a daily morning routine. Fumbling through task-laden processes is magnified when distractions such as being late cause a bag to be forgotten in the car or at home, or keys to be misplaced while absentmindedly walking and carrying on morning conversations with enthusiastic students who have anxiously awaited your arrival. Coworkers sharing their evening or weekend pastimes or answering the unexpected phone call can also cause distractions that lead to confusion and repetition and result in more wasted time.

As for making morning coffee and conversation, you wouldn't be asked to stop doing what it takes to get ready for or spending time with the people who depend on you! You are human, and you need to be comfortable, social, and content so you can get your job done. The goal is to look at what you do and make the process better, not eliminate actions that help you feel ready and prepared for providing quality service.

Based on the activities of entering the library listed above, what could be changed? Many things, but listed below are five quick fixes:

- Leave your keys in your nondominant hand until you are in the library and all doors are opened. This eliminates the number of times you place and retrieve your keys. In this example, you'll need the keys at least three more times in the next 25 minutes and your dominant hand will be lifting objects, opening and closing doors, while your nondominant hand can keep the keys ready for use.
- Get a larger tote bag that carries the contents of your tote, plus your lunch, and even a purse if you carry one (and be sure that what is inside each bag is essential, staying light and mobile). If you eat your own lunch from home daily, consider bringing multiple lunches at the beginning of the week so you only need to do this once every few days, if you have access to a refrigerator and you trust that it will still be there when you are ready to eat it.
- Carry your tote bag until you reach its final landing place, and take it there as directly as possible. This stops the placing and lifting of the bag multiple times.
- While at the refrigerator, place the lunch and remove the coffee while you are already standing there. There is no need to go back if you do this all at once.
- Put all of the coffee paraphernalia on a tray and bring it out in one movement, or just leave it next to the coffee maker.

Streamlining and refining the processes will help you shave off a minimum of three to five minutes by combining or eliminating steps when entering the door and help you perform the actions as a matter of routine that is distraction proof. It will help you get the day started with extra time to do things that really matter—and you are less than one hour into the day! With this practice under your belt, you are now ready to begin streamlining the library tasks.

## Preopening Routines

After entering the library and getting yourself settled, now your attention turns to the needs of your patrons, students, or teachers. Most likely, you will perform tasks such as turning on computers, copiers, lights. You may possibly need to remove cash from a safe or locked cabinet and place it into a register, check restrooms and exit doors, unlock gates, retrieve mail, and collect books from an overnight drop box. You may need to conduct a daily survey of the facility to check for anything unusual such as damage to the building or equipment in need of repair. You may want to check interlibrary loan requests and e-mail, and whatever else is a part of your preopening routine.

### *Document Your Process*

As you did with the "entering the library" routine, you should create a list of all your steps and dictate all the tasks you perform, as you perform them. Include everything it takes to be completely ready before your first patron walks through the door.

When you begin to document your preopening activities, note the location, the activities you perform including steps and start time, just as you did for "entering the library." Whatever you do, avoid trying to move faster than your normal pace. If tracking your actions slows your usual progress, causing you to miss any procedures that you would normally perform, include those actions at a later time at the end of your detailed list. You can do this from memory or wait until the "undone task" reveals itself when patrons ask for something that is not ready. Save those notes for later, when you have some time to analyze the process.

### *Map Out Your Tasks*

Later, or another day, get your working list of morning activities and where you are when you typically perform them. Now find either a map or the construction plans of the library. If you don't have access to professionally prepared plans, draw the space to the best of your ability. It doesn't need to be to scale for this activity.

You can draw your space by beginning with the front door and foyer. Then draw dedicated spaces that surround the foyer. After the foyer, note the location of the circulation desk, restrooms, break room, office, public meeting rooms, computer labs, makerspace, reading room, storage closets, and any other designated spaces as well as the contents of the spaces. The contents would include shelves, computers, printers, tables, copiers, and workstations, as well as doors and windows. To get a well-estimated drawing, if your ceilings are covered with acoustic ceiling tiles, the standard rectangular size is 24 × 48 inches. You can use 2 feet × 4 feet to estimate the size and shape of your space. After you have the walls drawn, include what is in the space that beckons your attention: the stacks that need to be straightened, the devices or machines that need to be powered, the areas where books are prepared for return to shelves, and supply stations that need replenishing. Make several copies of your drawing. Most likely, you will want to be able to draw on your map with an initial plan and then have a fresh copy to refine your activities later. A map of your space can be obtained either from architectural drawings, a drawing that is already available, or by creating it yourself. As seen in Figure 6.1, using graph paper and ceiling tiles will help you make a more accurate drawing, instead of just drawing it freehand.

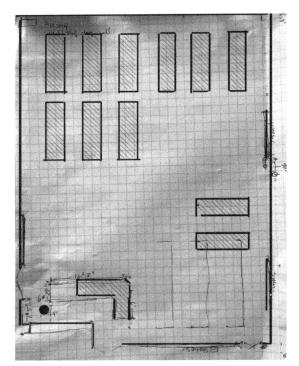

**Figure 6.1** Hand-Drawn Map on Graph Paper

### Begin to Analyze

With a map in hand, now you can mark the path that you took to accomplish your morning prep. Begin where you left off from your personal routine. Wherever you finished accomplishing your personal morning routines, either in an office, workroom, break room, or simply at your desk, that is where your floor routine will begin. You will chart

Change #2: Analyze Daily Routines                                              47

your steps with a pencil on the copy of your map. As you move your pencil around the space, jot down all the tasks that happen in the various spaces. You are probably unlocking, powering up, replenishing, removing, replacing. List any tools or supplies that you needed such as keys, paper, pencils, tape, clips. For example, if encountering an empty supply station causes you to return to a back office to retrieve supplies, if you need to unlock a door and you have to go back to your desk to get the keys, draw in that path that you took to return to another location to retrieve or access something that was left behind.

If you are now becoming acutely aware of how much backtracking and redundancy is happening in your process analysis, you may already begin to realize how simply reordering your routine or placing supplies or tools in a proximal location could save you lots of time and energy.

**Evaluate Remedies**

Not every idea that you have to fix your routine will be the real solution to your problem. Remember that professional engineers provide *potential* solutions to create *lean* processes for complex tasks. Granted, their suggestions, based on advanced math and experience with similar situations, will likely increase the odds that they are correct. But like a scientist, you need to regard the potential solution as a hypothesis. The initial implementation of the solution is an experiment. The outcome can be quantified by quicker times or reduced costs. If the results desired are not achieved, the scientist will go back and try again. You, too, should determine not to expect miracles with your first attempt at refining your opening routine and be prepared to rethink or refine your solutions.

Here are some possible solutions to timing problems.

- Turning on equipment takes time. Begin with processes that take the most time but can be completed without your intervention. Starting at a computer lab, diagnostics or updates can happen without you being there. If you do need to be present to click or flip switches between lapses of time, find other tasks to accomplish in the immediate vicinity so you can watch for prompts for the next action. It will be time saving to get other things done while you wait.
- There may be tasks that take more time if you set out to accomplish them specifically, instead of making them an incidental task accomplished along the route of a larger task. For example, if you sit at your desk and begin answering e-mails and then you discover that you need to get up to unlock restroom doors for your patrons, you have interrupted your e-mail answering time to stop and make a specific process of opening a restroom

door (retrieving your keys, walking to the restroom, unlocking the door, returning the keys to their location, and returning to your desk). This would take substantially less time if unlocking all doors is part of a morning route.

- You may be walking back and forth in a relay fashion trying to accomplish tasks. Instead, your route for travel should be a continuous line or a loop. For example, once you get long processes started, such as turning on computers that need time to update, you might then consider continuing with other tasks moving from the back to the front, or from left to right, or in a circle, throughout the library. One continuous direction—unlocking doors, gates, or compartments that patrons need access to during the day; turning on the lights; and checking on restrooms—can all be included in your morning routine, and as part of your circular or linear route will help you finish your tasks quicker.

- You could be backtracking to retrieve and replenish supplies from a different location than where they are needed. In a space that requires replenishment of supplies, consider moving the supplies to a cabinet in the immediate vicinity. If you don't have a cabinet there already, purchase a rolling cart or cabinet with a lock and key to keep essential supplies safe and close.

- You may have too many tasks to accomplish before you open the doors in the morning. If this is the case, consider moving some of the morning routines to the list of routines prior to close. If you feel that you have too much undone before you open your doors, it may be possible to move tasks such as filling interlibrary loan requests, replenishing copier paper, replacing periodicals with more current copies, or gathering door statistics to a later time of the day. But be careful not to fail to complete these tasks before closing. It is very difficult to recreate a list of reference questions answered, or recall important attendance statistics, or note a door count if it isn't done immediately. Playing catchup on tasks may cause you to fail to provide excellent service, so it is best to accomplish some tasks daily.

## Gathering Statistics and Other Reporting

There are tasks that take little time to do daily but can be quite time consuming when you put them off for weeks or months. Statistics gathering is one of those tasks that if documented as the event occurs, will save time from trying to recall or recreate vital information accurately.

There are tools that you can use to make statistics gathering easier to accomplish and efficient to report. For example, in-person reference questions can be counted with a standard tally counter like the one pictured in Figure 6.2.

Change #2: Analyze Daily Routines

E-mails or online chats can be accumulated in an e-mail folder labeled "reference," and then weekly or monthly, time can be spent transferring the numbers to a spreadsheet for reporting purposes. Or utilizing a form or survey that will transfer results to a spreadsheet will help to quickly gather statistics.

Circulation statistics can be gathered from your library management system, or circulation program monthly, or even analyzed at the end of the year.

Gathering daily gate or door count—the number of patrons entering the library—can be easily facilitated with an electronic door counter and traffic reporting software. The cost of the counter and the annual fee for the reporting are far less than hiring part-time staff to complete the task, and if you are the one to do the reporting, it frees you from taking measures to count people manually.

**Figure 6.2** Drawing of a Tally Counter

You can create a survey or form for each statistic that you are required to report, and you can access it easily from a desktop computer, or mobile device. Access the form with either a bookmark on your web browser or use a QR code to access it to make quick entries when the events are happening. Forms that produce results in a spreadsheet can be arranged to provide required information in the structure or proper format that is required by your library system. Cutting and pasting the spreadsheet results into a report without formatting will make reporting details quick and legible.

Attendance in the library, whether it is individuals or groups, should be gathered daily. It is important to account for patron type and number of people in attendance during library programs or special events hosted by the library as well as other events held in the library. Showing patron types (adults, young adults, children, families) and how many people are utilizing the library, as well as library services, is important to demonstrate the value that the community places on the staff and the facility. For school librarians, you may wish to keep an additional statistic of the time spent on duties outside of the library, such as lunch, morning, or dismissal duties. If you are responsible for troubleshooting technology problems, you will want to account for the time out of the library assisting teachers with these problems. If you are in a TV studio with students because you are in charge of morning announcements, you will also need to document that daily activity. If you are asked to cover for absent classroom teachers, it is imperative to quantify the time taken away from library service. If you attend planning meetings with your teachers, the time spent collaborating with teachers for instructional activities with students should also be accounted for, to demonstrate the amount of time it takes to provide quality instruction.

Nonroutine events, much like routine statistics gathering, are addressed most efficiently at the time of the occurrence. To handle these efficiently, consult with your governing agency or school board to help you locate policy and procedures that outline a prescribed process, so you can have it on the ready to document the irregular events such as accidents, altercations, or need for calling police or EMS. If there is not an already existing plan, ask that one be developed. When you have familiarized yourself, in advance, with a **ready form** for "incidents," there is no need to question or worry about what you should do or how you should document. When a patron is injured on the premises or suffers an event that requires medical attention, or if you discover vandalism, you must address this immediately. Additionally, if the police or an emergency medical service must be called, complete an incident report while the details are fresh in your memory. Approach your report with the mindset that your written words should not include judgment, speculation, or opinion. Be determined to be concise, writing only factual and objective statements, and don't forget to include your name and date.

## Circulation

Unlike your personal and preopening morning routines, or your statistics and reporting, the goal for the circulation desk is to streamline the processes that are conducted while in direct contact with your patrons. These are the actions and space changes that will immediately impact customer satisfaction.

The circulation desk is the heart of library operations. It is the primary location that sets the tone for interaction between library staff and patrons. It can be the point where the patron is served quickly and effectively, or where the patron walks away dissatisfied or upset with the service received. When you begin to analyze the activities, you will see that you can quickly assess and take steps to improve service and customer satisfaction at the circulation desk.

Paul Farris, in his book *Marketing Metrics,* defines **customer satisfaction** as "the number of customers, or percentage of total customers, whose reported experience with a firm, its products, or its services exceeds specified satisfaction goals." In a library, excellent customer service is achieved when the patron gets the information or materials quickly or returns materials that are handled accurately by a friendly, welcoming, and professional librarian. The patron may also require the use of the library space. It is imperative that the patron has a positive experience in a comfortable and functional library space.

Why is excellent customer service essential? As libraries are typically funded by a governmental agency such as a city, county, or school district, it is vital to provide the best customer service experience daily. When community members see a library as an indispensable part of their lives, they will do everything possible to ensure its continued funding. For this purpose, everything at the circulation desk should be what is needed to provide patrons the services that they are expecting, and nothing should be stored there that detracts from or prevents this from happening.

### Planning Phase

Before you begin a wholesale rearrangement of the circulation desk, you may find it beneficial to plan ahead of time by assessing essential activities for that desk and acknowledging what could be done elsewhere. In his book *Process Management*, James Riley outlines the formal planning process as follows:

1. Define the present process
2. Determine customer needs
3. Chart the process

First, because so many activities take place at the circulation desk, it is a good idea to identify all that happens at the desk on a regular basis by defining the purpose and scope of the processes that happen at the circulation desk. Address, for simplicity's sake, only the events that start with a patron entering the library and approaching the circulation desk.

Next, when you are attempting to define customer needs, Riley states that this will be "an ongoing, disciplined activity." You should be prepared to seek continuous feedback during the day-to-day activities of the library, noticing what your patrons require and how they participate in the process. Be ready to focus your remedies by creating mission and goal statements for each process and identify how "products," or in the case of libraries, books and information, move the process by creating a flowchart of activities.

To chart the process, each one should begin with "starts with" and finish with "ends with" statements, and you will want to include all the major processes in between.

Table 6.2 is what your initial brainstorming might look like when you define the circulation desk process and determine what your "customer" needs are on a regular basis in the library. The processes that are associated with the circulation desk begin with a patron entering the library in need of assistance, and the patron will express what those needs are either by inquiry or action.

Table 6.2   Identify Essential Activities of the Circulation Desk

| Starts with: Patron entering library in need of assistance ||||||
|---|---|---|---|---|---|
| Obtain/ renew a library card | Check out books | Pay fines, fees, purchase supplies | Return books | Reference Questions: Require access to materials | Referral Questions: Require directing patron to alternate service or source |

When you first begin to analyze the circulation desk, it is straightforward to list the major activities or processes that need to occur there, but so much more can be happening at this location, especially if you are a soloist. You might find yourself performing more tasks at the circulation desk than the ones that involve patrons, primarily because the circulation desk is literally the heart of the library. Because this is where most all activities or processes originate with the entrance of a patron, you find yourself at that location for the majority of the day, and you have other library management matters to attend to, as well.

To keep the analysis as simplified as possible, put all the other things that you do at the circulation desk on hold: checking e-mails for reference questions, processing books, preparing crafts for your next program, planning lessons, gathering materials for your next outreach event, or even eating your lunch. If you begin with a very general list of what

Change #2: Analyze Daily Routines 53

happens at the circulation desk *when a patron arrives*, you will have a limited number of processes to address. Limiting your targets for action will help increase your chances for success.

## Select One Process in the Planning Phase

Now is the time to "zoom in" on a process that you identify as a priority for your "customers." Perhaps it happens too frequently that your patrons, students, parents, or teachers insist that they have returned a book and you discover that they were correct: the book is on the shelf and is still on their account. This causes the person to be dissatisfied because now the account may include fines assessed and they do not want to pay. Even if you are a "no fine" library, having a book in arrears may upset the conscientious patron who went to great lengths to return it on time and now there is doubt. There are any number of scenarios that could have caused this error to happen, but regardless of the cause, a solution must be found to limit the number of instances that books are returned to the shelves without being checked in.

For example, children in schools sometimes think that placing a checked-out library book back on the shelves means they have returned their book. The error in the process is that the child did not first go to the circulation desk to check in the book. A teacher also had a habit of placing her checked-out book directly on a book truck of books that were already checked in and ready to shelve. In both of these instances, they both had books on their accounts that they believed they returned. A potential solution to the problem is to take greater measures to ensure that all books being returned to the library are checked in first, even if you believed that the existing process was already obvious.

Another issue could be that your response time in answering reference questions needs to be improved or that when people need help locating resources, there seems to be a lack of understanding of where materials can be found. These two events are so intertwined that it makes it difficult to be sure where to begin.

To dissect problems, you should create a worksheet to discover which process is a priority to you and your patrons and reveal what steps are involved. You'll quickly discover which are the simplest of processes to address that will achieve quick success, and then acknowledge the more complex process that will yield long-term results and greater time savings.

As you begin to elaborate on your initial worksheet, such as in Table 6.2, your worksheet might expand to look like Table 6.3. Look at the circulation desk and try to observe as an objective bystander all that

Table 6.3  Expanded Analysis of Circulation Desk Processes Based on Patron Entering Library with Need of Assistance

Starts with: Patron entering library in need of assistance

| Returns books | Needs New/ Renews Card | Asks Reference Question | Pays fines, fees, supplies | Checks out books |
|---|---|---|---|---|
| Approaches book return | Approaches desk | Approaches attendant sitting behind desk | Approaches register | Approaches check-out station |
| Drops books in book return | States need for card | Poses question | Explains situation | Presents books on desk |

Library Staff

| | | | | |
|---|---|---|---|---|
| Removes books from return | Requests alternate forms of identification | Ceases current activity to listen | Analyzes the situation | Requests ID number |
| Places books on circ desk | Examines documents for validity and currency | Fails to cease current activity to listen | Goes to register to assess fine | |
| Arranges barcodes | Requests other documentation | Has patron rearticulate or clarify question | Requests patron ID number | |
| Opens computer to check-in function on program | Opens computer to create or update function on program | Assesses the question | Opens computer to check patron status | Opens computer to check-out function on program |
| | | Knows the answer | | |
| | | Opens computer to database to search for answer | | |

| | | | | | | |
|---|---|---|---|---|---|---|
| Scans book | Checks other records to ensure other cards have not already been created | Directs patron to proper location | Walks patron to proper location | Enters ID number | Enters dollar amount | Enters patron ID number |
| Places book on desk | Checks for overdue fines or other fees | Patron leaves to search | Patron is successful | Removes fine from account | Accepts payment | Scans book for patron |
| Repeats process | Begins to fill out relevant information | Patron searches | | Removes book from account | Provides change | Repeats scan for all books |
| Places stack of books on truck | Confirms details with patron while entering information | Patron unsuccessful | Patron successful | | Provides receipt | Prints out receipt for patron |
| Organizes books with spines facing out | Generates account number | Patron returns | | | | Tells patron to have a nice day! |
| Sorts books on truck by Fiction, Nonfiction, Easy fiction, Easy nonfiction, CDs, DVDs, etc. | STOP! Will need to confirm data entered with patron, more process | STOP! This path leads to beginning the reference question process! | | | | Resets checkout to clear patron account |
| STOP! More processes for shelving books | | | | | | |

happens when a patron enters the library. The process begins with a patron entering the library.

Each of these patron needs will set a whole sequence of events into motion. If they are done efficiently, the event will lead to customer satisfaction. If they are done haphazardly or inefficiently, dissatisfaction will ensue.

When you begin to analyze the steps that are necessary to perform a task, you are engaging in **process decomposition**. Looking at every little step starting at a larger level, then getting down to the very minutiae of details will help you to streamline processes that are time consuming and preventing you from meeting your goal of improved customer service.

Table 6.3 is a look at processes at a macro level. This is a good first step to take before you seek to decompose processes and bring them down to their most efficient level.

Should you need to justify the use of your time, or present a formal proposal to be granted the time to analyze the processes in the library, Table 6.4 is an example of what to include in the proposal, including the purpose, scope, mission, and needs that will be addressed—separated by patron type and a summary of the goals you and your staff hope to achieve. You can prepare this document prior to your actual analysis of the circulation desk processes.

### Analysis of Circulation Desk Processes

Based on Table 6.3, you can begin to decompose processes or identify all the actions that are set into motion with the singular event of a patron entering the library: asking for a new or renew library card, reference questions, checking out books, returning books, paying a fee or a fine. Based on the initial identification of the library processes, and looking at them on a macro level, you might observe that answering a reference question is completed most effectively by listening attentively, explaining or providing information, and then finishing by walking the patron to the location where they might complete their research. Skipping the portion of the process where the librarian is tempted to sit at a desk and point to the general direction in an effort to get back to other tasks has helped you to successfully complete streamlining a patron-initiated process with little effort!

You might now also observe that just defining the main tasks involved in the check-in process is lengthy, and requires greater decomposition. Even though the trend in libraries is to have the patron check books out and in themselves, in many school and academic libraries, there are librarians who do not trust students to self-check their books. Therefore,

Change #2: Analyze Daily Routines

Table 6.4   Circulation Desk Process Analysis

County Public Library
USA

**Purpose:** The purpose of this study is to define processes that are currently performed at the circulation desk to maximize efficiency and provide quick and accurate service.

**Scope:** Processes address all services that patrons typically seek out from the circulation desk staff when visiting the library, including all actions that enable a patron to check in and check out materials, and obtain directions or reference questions. (This will not include reserving space for special events or programs provided by stakeholders or city services.)

**Mission:** It is the mission of the County Public Library Circulation Desk to provide high-quality library service with efficiency and personal attention to patrons; needs so they can acquire the materials, information, or instructions they need to be successful learners, readers, or users of library resources.

| Patron Type | Customer Needs |
| --- | --- |
| **Adult** | • Acquire a new or renew a library card |
| **Young Adult** | • Acquire a new or renew a library card (with adult present) |
| **Child** | • Acquire a new or renew a library card (with adult present) |
| **All** | • Check out or renew a book |
| | • Return books |
| | • Pay late fines or fees |
| | • Reference help, including inquiries about city services from other departments or local events |
| | • Inquiries about other services such as reserving library space, special programs, or activities held in the library |
| **Goal** | • To allow patrons to choose self-check or receive assistance in checkout and complete task in three minutes or less |
| | • To ensure that book returns are removed from accounts promptly |
| | • To accurately assess fines or err in favor of the patron (to promote goodwill) |
| | • To answer patron's questions accurately in five minutes or less |
| | • To provide contact information for questions that are outside of the scope of the library |

the merits of self-check warrants discussion. If you do not already employ some degree of a self-check system, you should consider the following scenario, as it is analyzed with a flowchart as illustrated in Figure 6.3.

The flowchart demonstrates how the patrons entering the library to return a book and deciding to either drop it in a book return or ask the librarian to address it immediately sets into motion a series of steps for the librarian. Bending and stooping, twisting and turning motions need to be executed to get a book from the return, to the desk to check in. Stacked up, cleared books are then placed on a book truck. Once on the truck, they will be arranged with the spines facing out, and then sorted into various groupings of fiction and nonfiction books.

In order to increase efficiency, a proposal is to place more of the process in the hands of the customer or the student. If you have not already employed self-check in procedures, you can see from the flowchart that

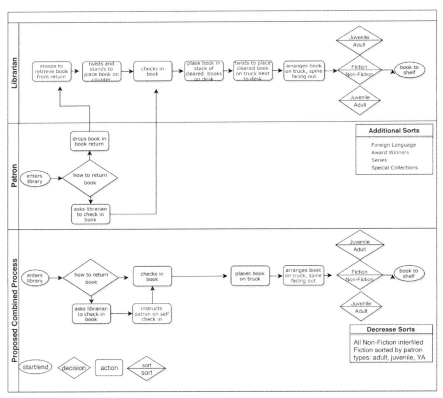

**Figure 6.3** Process Decomposition Checking in a Book

by simply having the patron check in their own books and place the books on a cart, at least four steps are saved for the librarian. These steps are repetitive and physical and include bending, stooping, standing, twisting, and lifting stacks of books every time a new patron enters the library with at least one book to return. An added benefit of making the patron responsible for the check-in process is that if a problem arises from a book being returned to the shelves without having been checked in, it is easier for patrons to forgive themselves for the error instead of forgiving a circulation desk attendant!

## Shelving

Because returning the books to the shelves is a process that happens as a direct result of the check-in, after streamlining the check-in process, we can save even more time by making the process of shelving as efficient as possible.

To do this, begin with an analysis of how you sort your books and other materials, and then you can implement some additional techniques that will expedite the replacement of materials to the shelves.

### Sorting Materials

The organization of the shelves determines the amount of sorting you need to do before you can take the books to the shelves and place them back where they belong. Adult fiction and nonfiction, juvenile fiction and nonfiction, young adult fiction and nonfiction; further dissected into genres in the fiction sections means sorting piles of materials into more piles before they can be organized by numerical or alphabetical order. Add the nonprint materials such as CDs, DVDs, kits, and even more time is spent sorting and preparing materials for return to the shelves. The more sections you have created to facilitate your patrons' ability to locate materials by browsing, the more time you will spend sorting and distributing, which may have the opposite effect of making it more difficult for your patrons to locate materials when they are researching!

This is not to discourage you from organizing your shelves by genre or gathering special collections. The message here is that if you are going to take the time to sort, be certain that the sorts that you make are worth your time and effort, and truly serve your patrons' needs. In a public library, for example, groups such as young adults and adults who read fiction greatly benefit from a collection that promotes browsing, as a library shelved by genre does. In a school library, if state award nominee books are important to your school because you participate in the selection process by reading and voting on those titles, your students will most likely benefit from having those titles located in their own dedicated space so they can quickly find and check them out. As the books are returned, you will be able to recognize, gather, and place them in their designated space instead of continually needing to interfile them with the rest of the collection.

On the other hand, if your teachers are better served by having all of your easy fiction titles in alphabetical order by author because they enter the library at the last minute with a specific book in mind that will bring to life a brilliant idea that will serve the needs of their students, or they are in urgent need of specific titles that support the curriculum that are written by a certain author, then sorting these titles by genre or special collections, would increase the amount of time needed to locate the titles, especially if the search now requires a catalog inquiry and your help directing them to the proper sublocation. Likewise, pulling nonfiction titles and grouping them by a theme or labeling them "scary" or "popular" or in some other subjective manner will foil a researcher's progress because they will need to search the whole collection, and then to search multiple sublocations until they can finally locate the book needed.

Using your best judgment of your patron's needs for browsing or researching, you will need to balance the time spent dissecting a collection into subgroups and sublocations with the certainty that the increased number of sorts into sublocations truly serves your patron's needs.

## A Technique to Expedite Shelving Books

Most often, when people prepare a cart with materials for return to the shelves, the process they employ is to:

1. Sort materials by their various subsets, such as fiction and nonfiction; and then
2. Sort the materials by As, Bs, Cs, and 000s, 100s, 200s; and then
3. Completely organize each book in shelf order on the cart; and then
4. Proceed to the shelves to take each properly organized book and place it directly on the shelf where it belongs.

*Consider skipping Step 3 to save time.*

*Change #2: Analyze Daily Routines*

In order to expedite the return of materials to the shelves, you can, after you check in materials,

1. Separate materials by their main subsets, such as fiction and nonfiction;
2. Sort and gather books by As, Bs, Cs, or 000s, 100s, 200s, etc.; then
3. Take the "chunks" of grouped books on the cart directly to the shelf and place them on the top of the shelf where they belong.

The placement of chunks of books near their proper location is called **staging**. Staging the materials above the shelf where they belong serves many purposes. It saves you time by simultaneously sorting and placing books directly near their proper location. It allows you to get the books in the vicinity of where they belong very quickly so there is only one location for a researcher or browser to look for a desired book. It also provides you the opportunity to return to the shelves with a stack of books ready to shelve later if you are unexpectedly called away to another duty. Furthermore, staging increases the odds that a volunteer will be able to return books where they belong by decreasing the number of locations where a book can be placed. Additionally, it helps to quickly clear out stacks of books from behind a book return station, which helps to restore the appearance of an organized library and an efficient librarian.

One thing to be certain about, when you use the technique of staging books, is that it is imperative that you follow through and complete your task of shelving materials at least by the end of the day. Otherwise you will have stacks of books piled up on top of the shelves and not on the shelf, and you would have just moved piles of disorganization from behind a desk to the tops of the stacks! This is not good.

To be able to utilize the library shelves as a staging location, the tops of the cases, or at least a portion of a shelf, should be kept clear. Though decorated shelves may be charming, excessive decorations placed on top of the shelves will keep you from utilizing the shelves as workspace and will impede your work. Unweeded shelves that are packed from end to end will also keep you from using the shelves to your advantage. This is an argument for keeping the shelves as clear as possible, where less is more and minimalism is the look you would want to achieve to help you serve your patrons better.

Most often, patrons who routinely visit the library will probably have returning of books as the first process they will engage in with you. This is likely the most time-consuming process in the library because the purpose of a library is for people to borrow and return books! So, focusing your efforts to improve the check-in process first, then utilizing the staging process to get materials back on the shelves quickly, will provide you with more time because you will be most efficient with the event that takes up so much of the day.

## Identify Small Problems That Affect the Big Process

When you are trying to improve on a larger process, you will have greater success when you are able to identify smaller obstacles that impede your ability to complete the task. For example, a soloist librarian may initially want to have many processes at one location, such as the circulation desk, because they are they only one there regularly to perform tasks. But some daily tasks can be involved, or very time- and space-consuming. When this is the case, that task should be removed from the circulation desk because it will become a time waster for the patron, volunteers, or the librarian themselves because they are continuously forced to work around tasks in progress.

## Material Returns

Observe how a patron returns books, which we know is an event that occurs all day, without notice at a public, special, or academic library, and all day *with* and *without* notice at a school library. Receiving and preparing books to be returned to the shelves is a multistep process that is exceptionally time consuming and labor intensive. Two things need to happen to make this process more efficient: first, the steps involved in checking in and placing the books to prepare them for sorting need to be streamlined and shared; and second, the process could be moved to a separate location so as not to interfere with other processes since that is an ongoing task for daily operations.

### *Create a Self-Check-in Station*

A good rule to follow is that if any processes can be shared with the patron, then it should be shared and the task should be kept at a separate location. Patrons can walk up to a dedicated station and scan their own book in and place it directly on a book truck. For a public library, this one change will eliminate at least four steps: lifting books out of the book return, placing them on a desk, scanning them in, and arranging them on a book truck to prepare them to sort.

School librarians can instruct students of all ages to also sort their own materials. So, if you provide two trucks—one for fiction and one for nonfiction materials, located next to a dedicated check in computer with scanner—students will have done half of the sorting for you. Even if there are some errors in the sorting, the number of books to sort will be substantially less.

### Proper Location of Tools, Supplies, and Even People

Any tools or supplies that relate to a task should be stored close by either in a storage cabinet or in storage under the circulation desk. Any other materials, such as supplies, that do not have a purpose in the execution of these tasks should be removed, relocated, or discarded. Similarly, if there are multiple staff members or volunteers performing certain duties, then ideally, there should be multiple locations for each or a couple of tasks: the reference librarian can also maintain schedules and booking of facilities; the circulation attendant can check books in and out, and receive payments; and a volunteer can sort and shelf books.

### Nonrecurring Events

There are so many other possible events that could happen in a library, but not routinely enough to warrant being called a regular process. Just as they say, "don't sweat the details," even when you are focusing on details to make your work life easier, there is a time and a place to draw the line on extraordinary events and simply focus on the regular, day-to-day activities of a library.

Once you have a general idea of the activities that will happen at the circulation desk, and you have tackled streamlining at least one of the processes, such as check-in and shelving, you may feel more confident to further analyze all the processes that happen at the desk. After realizing that not all of the events need to happen at the one location—and may, in fact, be more effective and productive at another location—you will be able to quickly identify the processes that would serve a patron better if removed and relocated to an alternate site.

## References

Farris, Paul W., Neil T. Bendle, Phillip E. Pfeifer, and David J. Reibstein. *Marketing Metrics: The Definitive Guide to Measuring Marketing Performance*, Second Edition. Pearson FT Press, 2010.

Montgomery, Douglas C., Cheryl L. Jennings, and Michele E. Pfund. *Managing, Controlling, and Improving Quality.* Wiley, 2011.

Morton-Owens, Emily G., and Karen L. Hanson. "Trends at a Glance: A Management Dashboard of Library Statistics." *Information Technology & Libraries,* vol. 31, no. 3, Sept. 2012, pp. 36–51. EBSCOhost.

Richards, Gwynne. *Warehouse Management: A Complete Guide to Improving Efficiency and Minimizing Costs in the Modern Warehouse,* Second Edition. Kogan Page, 2014.

CHAPTER SEVEN

# Change #3: Create Routines for Purchasing and Receiving

Keeping up with purchasing paperwork is one of those tasks that many people treat like weeding. Putting it off for another day, when you have time, is a mistake because the work that it takes to gather and match documents, resolve issues associated with a purchase, and then file the paperwork away in an organized manner takes more time than if you handled the documentation once, placing it in a file or a binder.

By spending a little time up front to learn an existing process for purchasing and receiving or, if one doesn't exist, by creating a reliable new process, you'll be saving much more time on the task of acquiring materials and services that will pay off far into the future. Following a routine with a checklist for documents and procedures that should be followed, or one that you design for yourself, will help to ensure that you complete all the necessary steps in a purchasing and receiving process. Just as importantly, staying organized with procedures and documentation of the process will help you make sound decisions on the materials that you choose to buy and vendors with whom you choose to do business. The greatest benefit is that you will be able to get orders completed quickly and accurately, which directly and positively impacts customer service.

## Understanding Accounting Controls

To engage in a regular, predictable, and effective purchasing process, it's helpful to understand why a process is even necessary. Because there is great responsibility in managing funds for a not-for-profit agency, creating a purchasing space that facilitates good decision-making, accurate record keeping, and efficient receiving of library materials, we will borrow best practices from accounting and bookkeeping.

## The Duties Associated with Fund Management

When you spend money for an organization, you enter into a **fiduciary relationship**. This means that you are being trusted to manage public funds for the library in a responsible way, as an agent of a not-for-profit organization, on behalf of the people in the community that you serve. You are expected to do whatever you can to make the best decisions possible when you buy library materials or resources, and it is your duty to add value to the greatest number of your community members' lives.

Building a collection that serves the people's informational and recreational reading needs effectively requires a dedicated space for material selection, purchasing, and safeguarding records. Knowing what to do to effectively purchase materials requires an understanding of the purchasing process.

## The Purchasing Space

Having a location dedicated to purchasing is important so you have the time and ability to focus on making thoughtful and informed decisions and a location to safeguard documents. Your personal desk is a logical location to facilitate these activities. The purchasing space should be free of clutter and have only what you need to work on the task of purchasing, as you learned about in Chapter 5. Most likely, you'll need a computer with Internet access and a document scanner if you are keeping all-digital records. Also, a locking cabinet for storing hard copies of documents will be necessary if your desk is in an open space. If you don't have a desk in an office that is separate from the public areas of the library, a locked cabinet is essential for proper accounting controls. A locked cabinet prevents your paperwork from being removed without your knowledge, plus the cabinet protects paperwork from damage or misuse. It also ensures that you'll be able to locate all purchasing documents quickly when requested by supervisors, directors, managers, or auditors. When you are organized and prepared with records, you inspire confidence in the accuracy of your work.

Keep hard copies of documents organized as you create them by having a three-hole punch or stapler available on or near your desk. A scanner will help you upload a hard copy into a digital file. These tools help

*Change #3: Create Routines for Purchasing and Receiving*   67

you to immediately prepare papers for safekeeping in a file of open or in-progress documents.

## The Purpose of Accounting Controls

Before we get into the details of purchasing, it may be beneficial to gain an understanding of accounting controls. Learning about the process of purchasing and why it has several steps that should ideally have separate people to perform them can help you to organize your documents, gather appropriate information, and know who to contact when purchases are at various stages of the purchasing process.

Strong accounting controls mean that when it comes to money, there should be different individuals or departments to handle the different activities associated with the purchase of goods or services. If there are not separate individuals responsible for creating a list or order, submitting the order to a vendor, receiving the items, or paying, fraud or theft might occur and go undetected for an extended period of time. Because of the possibility of big losses from theft, it is absolutely imperative that you keep all of the documents associated with purchasing together and easily accessible should you be asked to prove that you have been handling funds responsibly.

Even when there are different departments or people responsible for the various stages of a purchase, it is still important to take measures to verify that those steps are being completed accurately. The entire system of accounting controls should be set up so that no one individual has the ability to make purchases without another person knowing about it. It is, therefore, within everyone's right and duty to ask a purchasing agent to supply purchase order numbers; to produce verified packing slips from a vendor when orders are received; to share tracking information from the carrier (the delivery service); and finally, to verify that remittance has been made to the vendor for purchases.

Figure 7.1 shows the **source documents** that are created during the process of purchasing goods or services. Source documents provide details of a business transaction. The image also details the events that generate source documents and how you can file them. The source documents serve as the basis for journal entries that will be entered into the accounting system. As a result, all transactions occurring in the purchasing process are documented or accounted for in the formal accounting records.

Using a binder to gather source documents for purchases until the purchase has been completed is a great way to keep track of the status of an

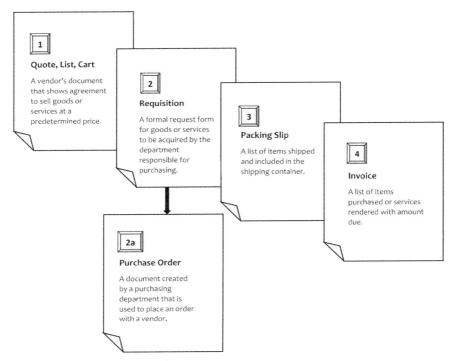

**Figure 7.1**   Organization of Source Documents

order. Prior to completion, the purchase is referred to as "open" or "in progress." A purchase is complete after it has been ordered, shipped, received, and paid. Only when the order is complete should you file it away both by fund source and by how the funds were used. The fund source can be from the annual budget, fundraising, or donations. How the funds were used could be for items such as books, supplies, processing, audiovisual materials, databases, technology, or furniture and fixtures.

Separating expenditures by fund and purpose helps to provide valuable information for future budgeting or allocation of funds to various departments or services. Similar to the term **expense**, which is used for businesses whose goal is to make profit from sales of goods or services, an **expenditure** is the term used when money is spent by a not-for-profit organization. Not-for-profit organizations include governmental agencies, religious groups, and charitable foundations, and a library within this type of organization. All of these entities follow the principles of fund accounting.

Expenditures are recorded in the accounting records when an obligation, which will be paid from current financial resources, has been incurred.

## Change #3: Create Routines for Purchasing and Receiving

The obligation to pay is only incurred after the goods or services have been received.

Maintaining a spreadsheet as a journal, with a running fund balance (money available for purchases), starting with the beginning fund balance at the start of the fiscal year, documenting encumbrances, and actual expenditures are important to facilitate responsible use of funds.

However, in account funding, the amount you initially plan to spend should be accounted for as an **encumbrance** until it is paid. An encumbrance means that a certain amount of funds, usually based on a quote, is reserved for payment. Encumbrances are used to prevent overspending the budget. It is not until an invoice is received for payment that the associated funds that were encumbered are then unencumbered, which means the accounting journal entry for the encumbrance is reversed or zeroed out. Then the actual amount of the invoice is deducted from the fund balance to keep a running balance of available funds.

The encumbrance and the actual expenditure may not always agree because sometimes ordered materials are not available, discounts may be granted later, or shipping costs that were not accounted for will be included. From a budgetary standpoint, you would prefer to see the invoice amount be less than the encumbrance. If the invoice is greater, there is risk of overspending the budget. Comparing the encumbrance with the actual cost minimizes the risk that funds will be overspent or highlights the fact that proper time and attention were not given to anticipating costs.

Vendors should do their best to disclose all associated costs with the purchase and delivery of their materials. When they have provided adequate disclosure, the risk of overspending the budget is minimized. Vendors that have been preapproved by your district or municipality should already be aware of the agreed-upon terms of sale and therefore should comply with those terms.

Separate accounting journals should be kept for each category of expenditure for which allocations have been made (such as books and e-content, databases, supplies, technology, furniture and fixtures). Each accounting journal entry should be numbered to reference a set of support documents that provide evidence of how funds were used.

Auditors can trace documents easily when you tie journal entries to source documents. Each journal entry can be **tied** to actual documents with a referencing symbol such as a letter or number, and that symbol will correspond to a group of documents with the same reference symbol. To tie accounting journal entries to support documents, simply handwrite your reference symbol on the accounting journal entry and then handwrite the same symbol on the first page of the stack of related source documents, preferably next to the total dollar amount. This makes it abundantly clear that the dollar figures agree and the balances on the journal entries are correct. Digital journal entries can be tied to digital folders with hyperlinks.

## The Purchasing Process

When it comes to **not-for-profit organizations** such as schools, public, academic, or special libraries (those entities whose goal isn't to make money but to provide service to people), you cannot be careful enough to make a clear and obvious trail of documents that demonstrate how you have managed and expended funds. Every organization that receives and spends money on behalf of the people it serves—from a small municipality to large school district, city, county, or state—should already have a clearly defined process for collecting and expending funds. Having procedures in place serves to protect the community as well as the employees who handle or manage the funds.

Someone with check-writing authority should not generate a check without first receiving a **requisition** (request for purchase), followed by a **purchase order** (a list of materials or services that is sent to a vendor), a **packing slip** (a list of the contents in a box or shipment), and **invoice** (a bill or statement that has an itemized list of what was sold and total cost of the sale, created by the vendor). Following clearly defined procedures helps protect everyone who participates in activities that involve money.

For example, a librarian who can authorize or initiate a purchase should not have the ability to sign checks to pay for the purchase or enter accounting journal entries that document the transaction. If one person can do more than one of these functions, this is called a **breach of internal accounting controls**. Keeping the purchasing and paying activities separate helps to avoid the **appearance of impropriety**. This means that everyone in an organization is taking all the necessary measures to make it obvious that library funds have not been mismanaged or used for any individual's personal gain.

One exception to the separation of custody and ability to initiate a purchase is a **petty cash fund**. Those who have custody of cash can authorize purchases in small amounts for minor emergencies. An arrangement such as this is permissible if receipts are retained as verification for the expenditure. Keeping receipts attached to a standard size sheet of paper with tape or staples is a good way to keep varying sizes of receipt slips organized.

Change #3: Create Routines for Purchasing and Receiving 71

Notations can be made next to or under the document describing what the petty cash funds were used for as they relate to events or purpose for which the money was spent.

### Formal Purchasing Processes

If you are required to maintain documents in a certain manner, then you definitely must follow the process precisely the way your governing agency mandates. You can ensure that you've completed all the necessary steps by creating a checklist of all the actions required. This checklist will help you to remember to follow up on each stage of the process for each purchase that you make, every time you make one.

Soloist librarians in large school districts or municipal libraries may need to complete a requisition, which is a formal request to a purchasing department to acquire certain goods or services from a specified vendor. When completing a requisition, you should provide all of the information that you are asked to provide. Doing so will ensure that your request is processed quickly and that you receive the items you are expecting.

### Informal Purchasing Processes

Soloists in smaller districts, private or charter schools, or small government entities may be given more freedom to make the purchases that they need without starting a formal request for purchase or approval process. If this is the case, even if requisitions are not necessary, it is highly advisable to create and save all documentation of a purchase to achieve transparency.

### Documenting Purchases

Adhering to a process, as well as archiving and storing documentation in an accessible location, takes resolve and deliberate measures to make sure that all steps are followed. You could always just start a purchase by submitting an order online, or beginning the paperwork and sending it off to another department, but if you don't take deliberate measures to document your work, you will quickly end up with piles of mysteries that will need solving every time you've lost sight of whether or not your merchandise is on the way or whether or not the bills have been paid.

Many purposes are served with a purchasing process that includes the organization of documents as they accumulate through the purchasing process. First, you won't need to waste time figuring out where you are in the purchasing process when weeks later you need to follow up on the status of an order. Second, keeping the documents will serve as proof that all goods and services are received in full and satisfactory condition, before any invoices are paid. Third, if your documentation is examined by either internal or independent auditors, all you will need to do is share the written procedures that you follow and your organized supporting documents that demonstrate compliance with those procedures.

With documents from every stage of the purchasing process, you will have created an **audit trail** with your records. An audit trail demonstrates that each step in the purchasing process was completed correctly. Moreover, it provides a history of transactions with objective and reliable evidence that good accounting controls over funds or resources were employed.

Keeping a digital file or folder for all documents that are generated when you regularly order online can include communications with the vendor about an order and any other relevant information that pertain to the orders you receive through e-mail. Hard copies can also be scanned and placed in the digital file so you can keep the storage of your records consistent. Ideally, you should keep either all digital, if you are permitted to keep records this way, or all hard copy if that is the preferred or required method.

The source documents to include in either a physical or digital file include items such as a list, quote, or cart; a requisition and purchase order, as well as the packing slip; and finally an invoice as described with Figure 7.1 and that will be further examined below.

### List, Quote, or Cart

A **list, quote, or cart** is the document that is generated when you have finished shopping and are ready to place an order. It has all the items you intend to purchase, including processing and MARC records, if applicable, at an expected price. You should also see terms of payment and delivery on the order. The payment terms are typically by credit card, purchase order, or check upon delivery. It may include shipping, handling, or freight charges, or the price net of discounts. You will need this document either to requisition the items from a purchasing agent, who will make the purchase for you, or you will use it yourself, to initiate the purchase of the items that you wish to acquire. In some instances, such as in private schools, where there is no purchasing agent, you may not need to create a requisition, but the order submitted directly to the vendor can serve as a support document at the initiation of the transaction.

## Requisition

If you need formal approval from a purchasing department in order to acquire goods or services, you will likely need to make a formal request for purchase in the form of a **requisition**. A requisition requires information such as item numbers, description, and price, and is submitted to your purchasing agent so they can purchase what you are requesting from the vendor. Follow all the instructions established by your purchasing agent, and make sure you date the requisition so you can determine whether or not you need to follow up on the purchase if it is taking longer than expected. The requisition should also be kept in a binder or digital folder, along with the list, quote, or cart of items requested, and attached as supporting documents. Your requisition will be the document that is used by the purchasing department to create a purchase order.

## Purchase Order

A **purchase order** is the document submitted to the vendor in lieu of the list, quote, or cart that you would have sent to the vendor directly when you do not have a purchasing department to handle the ordering for you. If you have a purchasing department, and they create a purchase order to place your order with the vendor, ask for or locate a copy to keep with your documents. The purchase order will have a number assigned to it that will be referenced on the packing slip as well as the invoice. If you frequently order from the same vendor, the purchase order number will be extremely important so you can keep track of invoices, especially when the original total cost of the order does not equal the actual invoice. Discrepancies can occur when the vendor can't fill requests because they are permanently out of stock, temporarily have items on backorder and you have elected to receive partial shipments, or they extend a discount that you were not anticipating. You may also have forgotten to include the costs of shipping, processing, or MARC records. The purchase order number will help you to track your orders to completion because you cannot rely on the total dollar amount being equal to your original order.

## Packing Slip

A **packing slip** is generated by the vendor and is placed inside a box or directly on the shipment. When you receive your shipment, you will need to verify that all materials listed on the packing slip are in the box and are the exact items that you originally ordered from the vendor. In addition to verifying that you have received all of the items that you have ordered, determine whether substitutions have been made. If substitutions were made, decide whether those items are satisfactory and are either of equal or greater value than your original choice.

There are times that substitutions are absolutely unacceptable, especially if you are ordering furniture or replacement parts for tools or equipment. If a substitution is not satisfactory, call the vendor to request a return authorization number and to get instructions on what procedures they expect you to follow to have the items returned.

You should be prepared to reject and return the shipment in its entirety. When you communicate your dissatisfaction from a position of indifference, the vendor's agent may be willing to do what it takes to remedy the situation without a return. Becoming too upset or irate may cause the vendor to become uncooperative, and then you may need to locate another vendor for future business. This might become a problem, especially if your budget is limited and you have little purchasing power, and the vendor has materials or prices that you need. If you are having trouble with the vendor, inform your purchasing agent so they are aware of the issue. This is important because first, they'll know not to pay an invoice because you are dealing with the vendor to get an order fixed. Second, they may be able to intervene and resolve any issues that you're having.

Only when you receive all materials that meet your needs should you give approval to your accounts payable agent or department to remit payment. Take the original packing slip and place your signature and state that you have "received materials in full and in good condition." Then make a copy of the packing slip and place it with your copy of the requisition; purchase order (if you have one); and original list, quote, or cart document. Then send the original packing slip to your accounts payable agent or department. The packing slip will be the source document, or evidence, that the agent needs to remit payment of the invoice.

### Invoice

The **invoice** is a document generated by the vendor at the time they have provided goods or services. You might receive the invoice in the mail or by e-mail on or near the delivery date of your merchandise, or it may go directly to your accounts payable department. If you receive the invoice prior to the delivery date, do not pay it, or give permission to pay it, until you have received your shipment in full and in satisfactory condition. Withholding payment until you have received all of your merchandise gives you leverage when making sure that the vendor completes your order to your satisfaction.

Change #3: Create Routines for Purchasing and Receiving       75

The invoice details the cost of the items you have purchased and any processing or MARC records for books and other resources if you have requested these services. It also includes shipping and handling, net of discounts. If you receive an invoice directly, make a photocopy or scan to create a digital copy of this document, and forward the original to your purchasing department. Most likely, your purchasing department will be invoiced directly and you will not have access to this document. Invoices should never be paid without the accompanying packing slip or acknowledgment from you that services have been rendered.

## Maintaining Records

Donovan Janus, in his article "Simplify Your Financial Bookkeeping." in the *Home Business Magazine*, recommends that you "spend 15 minutes once a week attending to financial matters. Make it enjoyable with a cup of coffee or tea, and then when asked to present your financial documents in an audit, you can produce work that shows that you are organized and transparent in your financial transactions."

If you cannot immediately address the paperwork as it is being created, make it a point to address your purchasing and receiving documents at least once a week, which is the next best thing. Always remember that the longer you wait to organize the documentation of your purchasing activities, the greater the risk that you will spend unnecessary amounts of time trying to recreate or remember information essential to complete transactions.

Table 7.1 is an example of a checklist with notes with important information about a purchase that also shows what process will be followed when a purchase is made. Ask the purchasing department for a document such as this, or create one for yourself so you can remain organized and efficient.

The information above the gray line is a quick summary of a "bottom line" for the entire transaction. It answers the questions "with this vendor,

Table 7.1   Purchasing Checklist

**Small Library—My Branch**
**Fiscal Year 20XX**

| Date initiated | Encumbered amount (quote) $ |
|---|---|
| Vendor name<br>Vendor ID# | Actual invoice                $ |

*(continued)*

**Table 7.1** (continued)

| Date completed/paid | Difference | $ |
|---|---|---|
| ☐ Itemized list (quote) attached | Special instructions noted | |
| ☐ Requisition completed/attached<br>Requisition number | Fund used | Account # |
| ☐ Requisition approved | | |
| ☐ Notice of shipment attached | Expected delivery date | |
| ☐ Packing slip attached | Discrepancies noted | |
| ☐ Invoice attached | | |

when did you start the order and when was it completed?" and "how much did you anticipate spending and how much was actually spent?" This is good information for you to evaluate the reliability of a vendor.

The information below the gray line features all of the steps that will help you create an audit trail. Along with the quote, requisition, invoice, and packing slip, it is also advisable to keep e-mails that indicate that your merchandise has shipped. Vendors usually provide tracking numbers so you can follow the order while in transit and make sure that you or someone will be available when the merchandise is scheduled to arrive. It also gives you a heads-up that valuable merchandise is on the way!

## Receiving Materials

An essential part of effective purchasing is the efficient and accurate receiving of materials. To ensure that you are literally "getting what you paid for," create a space where you can easily receive shipments, inspect and open boxes, and verify that you now have precisely what you expected to buy.

Especially when it comes to books, the receiving process should be done in a back room away from your anxious public who will want to check out those books the minute they see them! In your space dedicated to receiving and processing, have a table, cart, pencil, clipboard, and processing materials together. When you are done receiving, the next thing you may need to do is process them if they did not come processed or, at the very least, property stamp them.

At this dedicated space, verify that you have all of the boxes in the shipment and then locate the packing slip. For large shipments, determine how the packing slip is organized. Books may be listed in Dewey decimal order or author order or some other method. If the packing slip is organized in a logical order, try to remove the books from the box and place them on a book cart in the same order as the packing slip.

Small boxes can be placed and emptied from the table. Larger boxes that are too heavy to lift should be emptied from the floor while you sit on a low stool or are kneeling on the floor. As you work with boxes of books or other materials, you should take care to protect your back by not stooping, bending, or twisting your back as you remove contents from a box.

With larger shipments, organizing the contents of the boxes before you attempt to match the list on the packing slip helps to expedite the receiving process. With the packing slip placed on a clipboard you'll be able to move around the shipment and examine the materials more easily. However, smaller shipments need not be handled in the same manner. Simply placing a small number of books or supplies on the table and checking off the items on the packing slip as you identify the contents will suffice.

---

### Case Study

I am very fortunate to have access to a highly experienced professor of accounting. He holds a bachelor's degree in accounting, a master's in professional accounting, a juris doctorate, and practiced as an accountant and attorney for 30 years before becoming a tenure-track professor of accounting in the College of Business at the Texas A&M University in San Antonio. Gilbert C. Barrera, Jr., is also my brother. While talking about the writing of this book, I asked what he would advise librarians to do about documenting purchases on behalf of a library. He strongly recommended that all documentation be kept as accurately and current as possible. "There is no creative way to keep records," he stated. "Just use basic accounting principles and the organization of the records goes a long way in making a good impression on supervisors. But even more importantly, it makes a crucial impression on auditors."

Simply uttering the word "audit" strikes fear in the hearts of people everywhere. It makes them fear they will lose their job, be punished with fines, or be accused of wrongdoing. However, the professor stated, "As far as being audited [is concerned], that should never be a source of anxiety if everything is being accounted for and recorded as it should be. That all goes back to the timeliness [with which] the records are maintained. Being on top of it ensures accuracy and reliability."

Professor Barrera recalled an instance where a business manager was placed in charge of management and documentation of expenses by an owner of a business that was required to keep financial documents to report annual income to a manufacturer. The manager, even though he was following the orders of the business owner, allowed himself to be placed in a position that breached accounting controls. An investigation later revealed that the owner was using the manager as a pawn to misreport the income. Both the owner and manager were held accountable for the fraud. This example, though it did not happen in a library, highlights the consequence of not protecting one's self with proper accounting controls.

A librarian would not be responsible for such large amounts of money as a major corporation, but, he continued, "You would think that large municipalities would have [strong accounting controls], but any size entity can have a great deal of disorganization or dysfunction. The integrity of the accounting system isn't dependent on the size, it depends on those who are operating it. Even if you are not being watched, you should make it a point to keep good records because [if there is suddenly] a need to verify, the people in charge will be more inclined to blame the underlings."

When asked about a librarian who was "written up" by a manager for making a deposit that was "off" by less than one dollar—and the deposit was greater than the documentation—the professor stated, "[People need to] understand that materiality is based on the overall budget, and that it is subject to opinion. What is material to one manager is very unmaterial to another. But a dispute like that can resolved by referring to an accounting manual. The controller or whoever has the accounting function for a district, city, or county would have a manual that states how each account is to be used. There should be policies that are stated in black and white. You can even ask the auditors what dollar amount they would consider to be material, or what percentage of error is tolerable. Internal controls refer to having a defined procedure that ensures the integrity of the accounting information; that doesn't justify writing up someone for a minimal error."

## References

"Audit Trail." *Bloomsbury Business Library—Business & Management Dictionary*, Jan. 2007, p. 536.

Janus, Donovan. "Simplify Your Financial Bookkeeping." *Home Business Magazine: The Home-Based Entrepreneur's Magazine*, vol. 23, no. 1, Jan. 2016, pp. 17–18.

Rush, Elizabeth, and Gilbert C. Barrera, Jr. Interview. "There Is No Creative Way to Keep Records." Nov. 2019.

Spencer Pickett, K. H. *The Internal Auditor at Work: A Practical Guide to Everyday Challenges*. Wiley, 2004.

CHAPTER EIGHT

# Change #4: Create a Receiving, Processing, Repair Station

Create a dedicated receiving, processing, and repair station that is in a back room so it can remain set up and ready with all the supplies you need to quickly prepare materials for circulation. A three-purpose, dedicated station gives you the ability to go directly to the task and complete it without the need to set up before you begin and clean up after you're through. A continuously ready station helps you to get highly desired new books and materials, as well as much-loved older books, in the hands of patrons quickly and efficiently.

### Is Processing a Good Use of Your Time?

To clarify an important point, you may feel that you are saving a lot of money if you process materials yourself. Even though your invoice will reflect a lower cost without the processing, the reality is you are only saving money from being spent on a vendor, and paying the price by spending your time on processing. Finding the balance between processing in house and the amount of time you need to give proper attention to students, faculty, toddlers, children, young adults, adults, or professionals needs is imperative. If you regularly have time on your hands, with no people to attend to or planning to do, then doing your own processing is okay. But you'll need to evaluate for yourself how your time is best spent, and the message that you send when you decide to "do it yourself." If you have a budget that allows for a fair amount of acquisitions, it's perfectly acceptable to pay for books that are shelf ready, or negotiate to receive your MARC records and processing for free, especially when you are a soloist who is also responsible for providing programming, student instruction, and service to people. Remember that as a librarian, your core responsibility is to have one-on-one communication and excellent customer service with your students, teachers, parents, or patrons. So be careful not to commit to processing all of your materials yourself, unless, of course, your primary function in your library system is cataloger or processor.

### Justification for a Permanent Processing Station

Even if you buy your books shelf ready, a dedicated station is still necessary to receive new shipments of books, for property stamping or checking to see that the packing slip matches what is actually in the box. You'll also need a processing station for the occasional book purchased from a small publisher or bookstore that doesn't provide processing, or when you purchase materials at a conference. Also, you may receive donations that you would like to include in your collection, so these items will require your personal attention.

This station is also very valuable because it also serves as a repair station. Quick repairs such as replacement of jacket covers, spine labels, bar codes, and minor repairs of loose pages can be made effortlessly and get the much-loved books back into the hands of your patrons.

### Where to Place and What to Place on the Station

The best location for this receiving/processing/repair station is one that is not in a vital space, but out of the way. Because these tasks are best accomplished by you when the library is closed, when activity in the library is low to nonexistent, or when there is a volunteer to do the task for you—assuming you have already provided adequate training and supervision of the task before you assign it to be done unsupervised—you will want to locate it in a space where patrons are not being served.

### Processing

Several steps that may need to be accomplished to process a book include property stamping, bar code and spine label placement, radio frequency identification (RFID) tagging, label, or jacket covering. You may also want to place special labels on the books to indicate that they are new, that they are award winners, or that they are a certain genre.

## Bar Coding

Determine a uniform location to adhere a bar code on materials, such as in front or in back, parallel to the spine, either on the top or on the bottom of the book. When you first begin working in a library—when you are new to the facility—examine where all the labels and stamps have been placed and remain consistent with the placement. When materials have bar codes placed in the same general location, you will expedite the circulation and inventory processes.

If you can determine where bar codes and labels will be placed, consider how the material is shelved and what is the easiest way to access the bar code on the shelf with as little effort as possible. This is most likely the front cover, bottom or top left-hand side on the face of the book. Placing a bar code to run parallel, along the spine is ideal for right-handed scanning.

When you purchase books that are shelf ready, make sure, in advance, that your bar code specifications are on file with your vendors. Designate the bar code placement and give them a bar code sequence so that duplicate bar codes are not created by different vendors. You can make sure that bar codes are not duplicated by assigning each vendor a two- or three-digit number to be included in the sequence. A large, reputable vendor can advise you on the best way to do this.

## Spine Labels and Label Protectors

Determine a location for spine labels (e.g., .5 inches from the bottom of the spine) and commit to it. When you begin to process books, make sure you have spine labels already printed and ready to affix to the materials. Mark the location (distance from the bottom of the material to the bottom of the label) on the workstation or desk surface with tape or permanent marker. Be sure to place the measurements on the front and center of the desk so there is no need to reach or stretch to measure. Placing the measurements directly on the desk will spare you from wasting time reaching or searching for a ruler.

It is very convenient to keep spine label protectors on a multi-roll tape dispenser, such as one available from Demco or another reputable library supply catalog. A multi-roll, as illustrated in Figure 8.1, along with the rolls of tape, kept on the desktop, makes it easy to make books shelf ready.

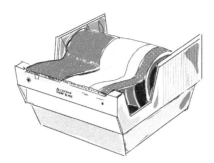

**Figure 8.1** Multi-Roll Tape Dispenser

Get a large dispenser that can hold single-faced, double-faced, and heavy-duty repair tapes, as well as spine and bar code label protectors conveniently on one dispenser.

## Property Stamp

Do your best to property stamp with self-inking stamps in locations that are quickly accessible to affix and remove when it is time to weed damaged, outdated, or superseded materials. Avoid putting hidden stamps in a book within the contents on a certain page number. It is time consuming to leaf through pages to both place and remove a property stamp and it does little to no good in discouraging theft. Title page and inside front cover are ample property-stamp locations. Do not use different stamps for different types of books, materials, or locations. Having to select the correct stamp for the correct material type is just time consuming and can cause confusion when volunteers are put to the task. If your weeded materials are recycled, then you may not need to concern yourself with removing the property stamp. Check your policy and procedures manual on what the procedures are for removal of materials. You will, however, at a minimum, need to scan the bar code to withdraw it from the collection.

**Figure 8.2** RFID Dispenser

## Radio Frequency Identification

If you use radio frequency identification (RFID) on your books or materials, you'll want to have necessary equipment and supplies included in the processing station, ready to use. An RFID dispenser such as one from Demco, as illustrated in Figure 8.2, can be mounted to a tabletop to make dispensing tags easy. Set up on a surface next to your processing station or directly on the station if it fits.

The quickest way to apply the tag is to affix it to the inside back cover of the book. Concealing it in the spine may not be possible for all books, so instead of creating a scenario where there will be exceptions, create a standard where there is plenty of opportunity for consistency. Anyone determined to remove RFID tags will not be deterred by a concealed tag, so you might as well just place it where it is easy for you to access.

### Jacket Cover Dispenser

There is a great benefit from having a jacket cover dispenser ready for use on the processing station, as well. A

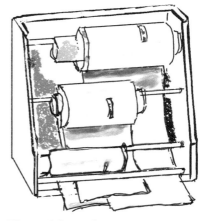

**Figure 8.3** Jacket Cover Dispenser

dispenser, such as the one in Figure 8.3, makes it quick and easy to measure out a length that fits your book jacket and saves you time from pulling the materials out of storage, cutting the length, and then returning it to its proper location. This dispenser, also from Demco, keeps rolls of jackets from falling off the table when you pull, and keeps them "stacked" in one location, which means less counter or table space is used.

The presence of a jacket dispenser makes a clear designation of the purpose of the space. It says, "This is a processing station. A necessary space in the library." If you are in a school library and the principal is looking for space to convert to an office or for storage that is not for your use, a jacket cover dispenser, along with all of the other processing materials that surround it, makes a clear statement that this space is not available for use for a nonlibrary purpose.

Keeping the minimum number of jacket covers on hand saves space on your dispenser and money when it comes to ordering and shipping costs. To do this, purchase the largest, a medium size, and smaller size roll for jacket covers. Three sizes should accommodate most all books that require jackets.

9"—for most all fiction, novels, children's books

12"—for nonfiction and textbooks

16" or the largest roll you can find—for all others

Always use the smallest-sized roll of jacket covers first to minimize costs, and purchase more of the smaller sizes than the larger ones. Begin with two rolls of the smaller size and one of the larger. Write the date that you purchased the rolls on the inside of the cardboard tube to determine how long it takes you to use the roll. Reorder quantities based on how quickly you use the rolls. If you use one size much faster than the others, then order multiples of that size. Balancing out the quantities that you purchase will ensure that you have the materials when you need them, and that you are not storing excess quantities of materials that you don't need.

### Make the Station Complete

Along with your materials such as labels, label protectors, bar codes, spine labels, jackets, and tape, don't forget to include scissors, a box cutter, and ink for self-inking stamps. And if you ever have the ability to purchase a table for processing, select one that is at a height at which you can stand and work, or choose an adjustable table that raises and lowers so you can stand or sit and work at an ideal height that preserves your back and neck. Don't forget to purchase a stool for single-height tables. Paying close attention to work surfaces that adjust to your needs will save you from injuring your neck, back, and shoulders while you work, and it will give you the option to either sit or stand for marathon processing sessions.

### When You Have Little Space to Spare

If you are operating a small but efficient library, you can still create a processing station that is separate from your circulation desk. You can achieve this by placing your processing materials on a multileveled cart or short cabinet with wheels. By making your station mobile, you can bring it out to work on your processing, repair, and receiving tasks and then roll it back out of the way to a back office or storage room when you are done or when you have patrons who need your help or are in need of the library space.

---

### References

"Procedures Manual." University of Arizona, College of Law Library. www.law2.arizona.edu/Library/ProcedureManual/Index.html

Richards, Gwynne. *Warehouse Management: A Complete Guide to Improving Efficiency and Minimizing Costs in the Modern Warehouse*, Second Edition. Kogan Page, 2014.

"What Are the Standard Book Sizes in Publishing?" *Reedsy Blog*, Oct. 26, 2018. blog.reedsy.com/standard-book-sizes/

CHAPTER NINE

# Change #5: Implement Procedures for Effective Communication

When handling reference questions with the public, your patrons, or stakeholders, creating routines for answering in-person, phone, and e-mail inquiries will help you to respond quickly and effectively.

Your role as a librarian is twofold. You are a provider of materials and space, but most importantly, you are a provider of reference and instructional services. How you handle your reference work can make your patrons either very satisfied or extremely dissatisfied. For this chapter, we should consider our patrons or stakeholders as "customers," because employing best business practices of customer service is the goal.

Customer service, from a business perspective, is the key element that can either make a business profitable or cause it to fail. Attentive or responsive service leads to repeat customers who refer new customers to the business. Positive reviews by word of mouth or social media mean the business spends less time and money on advertising or promotion to attract new customers and gains more opportunities for the business to be profitable. Poor service leads to drops in sales, plummeting stock prices, and at the very end, financial ruin.

But how do profit and financial ruin relate to libraries? A library's purpose is definitely not to be profitable; it is a public service. Libraries seek to provide books, materials, and information, and space for the people it was built to serve: either citizens of a municipality, students in a school, or professionals in an organization. What does this mean for a school, city, county, or state librarian? Well, no one appreciates hearing this from patrons, especially when they are angry and raising their voice to you, but your salary is in fact paid by their taxes. Stakeholders expect a good return on their investment, and even though you are not beholden to any one individual, you are still obligated to provide the best customer service that you can—with a smile.

Your goal is to have patrons leave the library feeling like they were important enough for you to stand up and spend time addressing their information needs, that they were welcomed enough to spend time in the environment, and they are convinced enough to feel that if the library didn't exist, it would be a detriment to their well-being. When you have done your job correctly and efficiently, that person is ready to go out into the world to tell all their friends how wonderful their library experience was that day.

If you aren't yet convinced that you need to provide excellent customer service, consider what is at risk if you don't. By not working to serve your customers, the public perception is that the service is of little to no value. When budgets are tight, there would be no remorse for cutting library funds. When allocations for salaries and materials are cut, the lack of staff and resources renders you even less able to provide quality service. Because of the potential to fuel a belief that libraries are expendable, it is your duty and in your own best interest to provide the most excellent customer service and programming that you can, every day.

If you are a soloist, the face of customer service is only you. There are multitudes of ways a library patron can reach out to you, so there is a challenge to balance or manage all the different ways of responding to inquiries. A stakeholder can arrive in person or contact you by e-mail, phone, and whichever social media you have chosen to utilize. In order to provide the best customer service that you can during these patron/librarian interactions, it's important to place yourself in the library, where are you are visible and appear to be ready to help.

Having procedures in place that will help you increase the odds of providing excellent customer service in the least amount of time is important. Establishing a location and creating processes to manage your patrons' needs will increase the odds that when someone reaches out, they feel they were given the attention they deserved. Also, when they walk away with the information or materials that they were looking for, they were able to walk away with an experience that was satisfying and enjoyable and has them looking forward to coming back again.

## When You Must Work Away from the Desk

No matter what kind of library you are responsible for, people expect to find librarians at either a reference or circulation desk. But when you are a soloist, responsible for a multitude of tasks, that's not always possible. If you need to work in a back room or in the stacks during library hours, be sure you either have the ability to see or hear the door opening or place a door-open chime at the entrance so you will know when patrons have arrived. Once you hear the bell, go greet them.

Likewise, when you're working in a back office, place your desk so when you're seated you're facing the door and have a view of the foyer. And if you need to work on projects in the main library space, keep a separate table or space for those tasks, behind or away from the circulation desk. This is especially important when you are using scissors or box cutters and there is a chance that a young child, or someone with malicious intent, will enter the room. A table or cart on wheels is ideal so you can push the project materials out of sight or into a safe location when your patrons arrive.

If you are a school librarian and you are working with a class or a group of students, be certain that you have a good line of vision throughout the facility from both the circulation desk and your instructional space. This is imperative so that students who are in the library for self-check or during free circulation hours have adequate supervision even while you are busy teaching a class or working with individuals or small groups. A clear view of the front door, from all directions of the library, will make certain that both you and the visitor are aware of each other's presence.

## Policies for Answering In-Person Reference Questions

It's important to address how we interact with patrons, primarily because most everyone has had a negative experience with a customer service representative. Maybe even you inadvertently have been an unwelcoming presence at one time or another. If you are at a desk, concentrating on paperwork, or cataloging, or planning, you may look agitated when you stop to answer a question, especially when you have reached a state of flow in your work. But the worst thing you can do is make your stakeholders feel that they are inconveniencing you. No one can deny that your core responsibility is to help people when they ask for help. So, creating personal policies for handling in-person reference questions that will help you help your patrons are as follows:

1. Always acknowledge the person who is approaching or standing in front of you. Remind yourself that if someone has decided to make the library visit their priority, you must make it your priority to acknowledge their presence and offer assistance. No matter what your role is in the library, as a person who is paid to work with and for the public, it is your job to be present to the person who has made the effort to ask a question face-to-face.

2. Abandon any other task immediately as long as you can do so safely. Put personal calls on hold, stop conversations with a coworker or a friend who is visiting with you. If you are cutting paper in a back room for story time, put the scissors down and walk toward your patron who is waiting for your help. If you are standing on a ladder and hanging decorations, tell the patron, "I will be right with you!" At that point, anyone would understand that they should give you a minute so you can safely come down.

3. If questions or requests require another person's expertise or the resources of another library, clearly state that you are prepared to take measures to either locate an expert or search another library's holdings. If you consult with an expert, before you hand off the patron to someone else, explain what the patron needs so they do not go through the frustration of explaining again to another person. If you need to request materials through interlibrary loan, ask for the patron's library card number and help the patron learn the process so he or she can complete a request independently the next time. You'll also need to determine if the patron is willing to return at a later time or date when the materials arrive. Be certain to get a phone number or e-mail address so you can contact the patron if your library information system doesn't already have the ability to contact automatically.

    When you make contact, use the opportunity to recommend the library services that you provide that help people get what they need. Services such as making requests for books via interlibrary loan, online catalog features such as placing a book on hold or calling by phone to request a book ahead of time, will help to ensure that the trip to the library is productive for the patron. If phone calls or Internet from home isn't an option, then be sure to make it clear that everyone is welcome to come in and explore at any time—especially when the trip to the library is a recreation or pleasure for the patron!

4. If you are working with a patron and the phone rings, if you have voicemail, let the phone take the message. If you do not, excuse yourself from the person in front of you and answer the phone. Chances are it will be a quick question about hours or days of operation or about upcoming events. After you address the quick question, you may return to your in-person patron. If the phone question is more involved, ask the phone person to hold; if you

are almost finished with the in-person reference question, then get back to the phone. When you have finished with the phone inquiry, be sure to go back and check on your in-person patron—to make sure they are being successful. It may sound like this requires a bit of juggling, but once you get into the habit, it will become easier—almost second nature to you.

## Policies for Handling Phone Reference

In an article by Susan Ward on the website *The Balance Small Business*, she addresses time-saving tips for handling phone calls.

1. Use a professional phone greeting such as "Our Town Library, Elizabeth speaking. How may I help you?" This tells the caller that they've reached the library and they may now tell you exactly what information need you may serve. It "puts the onus on [the caller] to answer the question," and saves the caller time by eliminating the need for exploratory questions such as, "Is this [the library?]" and it dismisses the opportunity for "idle chit-chat."
2. Determine if the call can be answered now (e.g., questions about operating hours, rates for overdue fines, upcoming programming details) or if it is "more complex." If the answer will take some time to find, ask for a phone number so you can call back when you have more time to devote to arriving at the solution, or extend an invitation to visit the library in person.
3. Stop chatty conversations by paraphrasing questions or summarizing the answers. Ward recommends the use of phrases such as "So what I hear you saying is . . ." or "So the key points are . . ." or "Is (insert summary) a fair summary of what you were asking?"
4. "Close each call with a summary of the action you and the caller have agreed on." When it comes to reference work, you may wish to repeat procedures for accessing the library catalog, databases, or what to bring when applying for a library card. A quick summary of the call doesn't take much effort on your part, and this step helps your patron achieve her or his goal without confusion or frustration due to missing critical steps.
5. "Keep a message pad by the phones, so you can jot details during the call." Ward states, "This is not only good time management, helping to keep you focused on the call, but a help to time management later if you need to find and/or review the details of a particular conversation." Additionally, if the phone call results in some key information that you will find useful later, transcribe the notes onto a digital document that you can file in your drive, especially if it pertains to ongoing matters or is information that others in your organization will benefit from revisiting. Do this immediately, as randomly jotted notes seem to become indecipherable hieroglyphics when they've been sitting on a desk and read later, totally out of the context of the conversation that generated them.

6. Use technology to manage phone calls when you are unavailable. If you are suddenly overwhelmed with patrons at peak hours, while running a program, or before, after, or during lunch hours, you wouldn't want missed calls to go unanswered. Schedule a time when you will return all missed calls. By responding to unanswered phone calls at once, you will save even more time.
7. For frequently asked questions (FAQs), keep a written script posted by the phone or on your computer desktop. This will save you time by eliminating the need to search for answers or to think about how to answer a particular request when answering the phone.
8. Give patrons and vendors an e-mail option. Most people prefer to e-mail when they can. It is good for both parties because there is a written documentation of instructions or information that they may refer to in the future. Ward recommends that you provide your e-mail address on your business cards or library website in a prominent location so you can be sure to improve communication.

## Policies for Handling E-mails

E-mail is another access point for communication between you and your patrons. The beauty and the sorrow of e-mail is that messages stream in all day—and night—long. For your sake and sanity, you will probably want to schedule e-mail answering time, just as you do for your return phone call time. To save time responding to e-mails, you will want, as you did with phone calls, to front-load certain tasks by planning out scripts that can be reused and to schedule time early in the morning and then later in the afternoon. If you receive an abundance of e-mails throughout the day, you might consider revisiting them when you have no other pressing matters.

An article in *Inc. Magazine*, "How to Use E-mail to Improve Customer Service," addresses the efficient handling of e-mails. Helpful suggestions include:

1. Be brief and make your message easy to read. Start with the most important information and use bullet points to make the message easy to read. The subject line should literally address the contents of the e-mail, making it easy for the recipient to search their e-mails at a later date.
2. Respond as quickly as possible. Try using an automated response, such as, "Thank you for your inquiry. A librarian will be responding to you as soon as possible." That lets the patron know that their question is in your inbox and you will respond as soon as time permits.

3. Solve your patron's problem as quickly as you can, and if you can't find an answer or a solution, consult with an expert right away. Tell your patron that you are taking actions to find an answer, and when you get answers, always give credit to your source. While you don't want to waste time trying to figure things out, when you have tapped someone else's knowledge, you should let your patron know where the information came from.
4. Consider sending a follow-up e-mail if you are uncertain if the solution you offered did in fact solve the problem. This is your opportunity to learn from the process, so have a survey ready that provides direction for professional growth for you.
5. Turn the contact into an opportunity. Now that there is correspondence with the patron, ask if he or she would like to receive an e-newsletter about future library events and programs.

In addition to the above recommendations, here are some time-saving shortcuts to answering e-mails.

### Create E-mail Templates

Some types of e-mail messages are common, and tend to be rewritten and sent frequently. To save time and be more productive, create templates of common e-mail responses that can be personalized. You can personalize the response with the patron's name and any other unique information as needed.

### Use Auto-Responding Messages

These are the automatically generated responses you send when you go on vacation, explaining why you won't respond to e-mail immediately. You can also use an auto-respond message to confirm that you received an inquiry e-mail and when the sender can expect a reply. This is a good strategy to use instead of letting several days pass without responding.

### School Libraries: In Person, Phone, and E-mail

School libraries enjoy the fact that your patrons (your students, teachers, and parents) have a greater likelihood of returning for what they need because the library is so conveniently located and you have the ability to continue communication to ensure that they get the service that they seek.

When it comes to in-person inquiries, there are an infinite number of "emergencies" that can happen. For both students and teachers, they tend to arrive in person, in need of immediate assistance, for example, when someone has forgotten to check out a required novel, when a teacher is unexpectedly asked to cover a class for someone else, or both are just simply not prepared. It has happened to everyone at one time or another. If it happens too frequently, it is very tempting to say, "an emergency on your part does not constitute an emergency on my part," but you must resist the urge and do what you can to help.

If you are not responsible for a class at that moment, you should drop what you are doing and assist in locating resources or help them get started with working independently and check back frequently.

If you have too many people in need of your help in front of you all at once, you'll need to prioritize the emergencies. Get the most emergent started working independently first, and then write down the names of students with less pressing problems. Invite the students to return later when there are fewer people needing help—maybe before or after school. As you wait for their return, you can either do a preliminary search to find answers for difficult questions, get prepared with potential resources when the student returns, or have books pulled and ready for recommendation. If the student doesn't return, you have the luxury of being able to call the teacher and ask if the student will be allowed to return to the library during class, if it is convenient.

You can do the same for teachers who need emergency library materials. It happens quite often that a teacher may be on a break or they are using their planning time to gather materials. If you are able, stop what you are doing to help. But if you are occupied with a class, ask them to leave a note or e-mail the request, and you will get materials pulled for them as soon as you are able. The teacher can then return at a later time, or better yet, you can call their classroom and ask the teacher to send a student to pick it up.

In schools, it is best to teach your community how to avoid the in-person, emergency situations to begin. When it comes to assisting with gathering library resources, having a preferred procedure in place for your teachers works because you are circumventing the conditions that cause teachers to race into the library in a panic. Plus, everyone on a school campus, including yourself, may be busy with a class or individuals, making it difficult for you to drop everything and sacrifice the quality of the lesson for the students sitting before you.

You should make it very clear that if you are available to help, you will. But making requests ahead of time, by e-mail or through your library management system, will enable you to fill requests for materials and

## Change #5: Implement Procedures for Effective Communication

have them already checked out and ready for pickup. Inform your teachers of your schedule for checking e-mails for requests and stick to it! The best time to check e-mails might be first thing in the morning for a midday pickup and one hour before the end of the school day for those who will be picking up first thing in the morning.

Be sure to provide training on the system you would like to implement for the whole group at a faculty meeting so they are made aware of your service and procedures, and then be prepared to train individuals one-on-one, as they will not remember the procedure the first time they are in need of your help.

Refer to your library management system's instructions on how patrons can create resource lists or put materials on hold. Ask friends of all skill levels (those who are comfortable and those who are not comfortable with technology) to test the procedures for you to determine if it is easy enough to manage. If it is, then utilize the system that is already in place. That will save you time. If it is not intuitive for the user, then consider devising a different method that you will employ, such as e-mailing titles or copy and pasting catalog results into an e-mail. Be sure to ask for call numbers of the materials that your teachers want, explaining that if you have the call numbers, that expedites the retrieval process for you and the availability of the materials for your teachers.

When you present this procedure to your faculty, be certain that you feature it as a time-saving, convenient procedure for the benefit of the teacher—not for your own personal convenience. And be sure that the procedures you have put in place are in fact as easy as possible or your potential users will not be willing to participate.

Remember that time management requires that you organize, prioritize, and implement action plans. You will need to be prepared to utilize your critical thinking skills and make instant decisions on how to best serve the people who contact you for help, either in person, on the phone, or by e-mail if you want to provide excellent customer service. While soloists have many different responsibilities, it is important to remember that your patrons come first. Managing your time and space well keeps you alert and aware of your stakeholders' presence, and having routines in place for handling reference questions will help you to achieve your goals of keeping yourself and your patrons happy and the service you provide will be acknowledged as indispensable for your community.

## References

"How to Use E-mail to Improve Customer Service." *Inc. Magazine*, www.inc.com/guides/cust_email/20909.html

LII Staff. "Non-Profit Organizations." Legal Information Institute, June 15, 2017, www.law.cornell.edu/wex/non-profit_organizations

Miller, Ian. "Time Management Skills for Customer Service Managers." *CSM—Customer Service Manager Magazine*, www.customerservicemanager.com/time-management-skills

"Public Service." Definition. Merriam-Webster, www.merriam-webster.com/dictionary/public service

Ward, Susan. "Here Are Some Helpful Time Management Tips for Incoming Phone Calls." The Balance Small Business, www.thebalancesmb.com/time-management-tips-for-inbound-phone-calls-2947334

CHAPTER TEN

# Change #6: Manage Storage and Reordering of Supplies

Small libraries mean tight budgets. Large libraries with recently reduced budgets will also need to rethink the amount and timing of how funds are expended. Wise use or distribution of your funds is essential. You could easily reduce risks of running out of important supplies by over-purchasing items like pens, pencils, paper, processing materials, printer and copier toner, and keeping well stocked with whatever it is you need to run your library. But if you have limited space, are required to justify spending, or in need of regulating your spending to keep funds available for the unexpected instead of on the shelves of your storage or in the hands of suppliers, you'll find it helpful to actually *manage* your supplies and reorders. Inventory management strategies as well as utilizing simple formulas and calculations will help you to complete reorders of materials and supplies in both an efficient and fiscally responsible way.

## Where to Locate Supplies

Where you store supplies in the library can have a bearing on efficiency and control waste. A central location of supplies is essential for a large organization, mainly to monitor for waste or theft. But when you are a soloist and the only one accessing the materials, you can place materials in optimal locations: close to where you need them and where you can monitor your supplies on hand as they are consumed. Strategically located cabinets or storage that is under lock and key is ideal for placing materials near where they are needed most.

For example, reams of paper can be kept in a cabinet under or next to a printer, along with the accompanying toner cartridges, staples, and copier cleaning supplies. In a makerspace area, rolls of filament for 3D printers; materials for laser cutters; all related craft supplies such as markers, crayons, papers; and whatever else you provide can also be kept in a locked storage closet or cabinet in the same room or space so it is ready to replenish when necessary.

When you keep the materials nearby the location of need, you are sure to notice when supplies are running low and can place an order when you reach the **reorder point**. Reorder point is a predetermined number of supply items remaining that signal the need to purchase more. Reorder point is calculated by considering the amount of time it takes to receive a delivery and the amount of materials that will be used while you are waiting for the delivery to arrive. The amount of inventory that is kept in case the order takes longer than anticipated or there is an unexpected amount of demand is called **safety stock**.

Why would you want to arrive at this optimal reorder point? Imagine how frustrating it would be to a patron who expects to find a copier ready to use at the local library and then discovers that you are out of paper. Now the patron will need to go somewhere else to get the work completed. Inversely, if you purchase an overabundance of paper, you will find yourself moving heavy boxes of paper that are in your way or taking up precious storage space. You also run the risk that your cleverly stored paper can be lost or forgotten, and then you are unwittingly reordering even more paper! Worst-case scenarios include suffering an unexpected water event such as a broken pipe or leaky roof that damages your entire reserve of paper. By spending precious funds on an oversupply of any type of material, you may end up preventing yourself from acquiring other supplies for children's or teen programs or events, reading celebrations, or hiring guest speakers or performers.

## Calculating Reorder Point

If you take some time to monitor your past purchases of copier paper or other materials that you and your patrons use on a regular basis, you will reach this ideal point of having what you need when you need it. We can continue to use the example of copy paper to learn how to do this. You will need to observe two things about your paper usage:

1. The length of time it takes to use a single ream or case of paper. (Use a case if paper usage is extensive.)
2. The amount of time it takes for you to reorder and receive paper.

Change #6: Manage Storage and Reordering of Supplies

If you can drive to the local office supply and return with the paper during your lunch break, you wouldn't need to worry about the reorder point nearly as much as you would when you need to create a requisition for a purchasing department to place an order for you and then wait for the vendor to deliver the supplies. If your school district or municipality has a warehouse or provides supplies upon request, that too would change the lag time between needing and receiving of supplies. **Lag time** is a delay between tasks that have a dependency, and in the case of the paper order, the time between the order and the receipt of the paper supply.

To make sure you don't run out of paper, you should focus on creating some **lead time**, or overlap between the tasks that have a dependency. This means that you should order the supplies at a point when they will arrive just before you run out. You can anticipate the amount of inventory of supplies and materials you will need to reorder by asking the following:

1. How much of a certain supply item, such as reams of paper, do you ordinarily use in a day? (Average daily usage.)
2. How long does it usually take for you to receive a delivery once the order has been placed? (Lead time should include days to process a request for purchase, days for fulfilment, and delivery.)
3. On a day when there was an exceptionally large use of a material (such as paper), how much was used? (This amount will be your "safety stock.")

Average daily use can be obtained by making a conscious effort to observe the usage for a period of time. At any point in time, observe how many items are used in a day for about 5 days (either consecutively or randomly in a month). Add up the amount used (in terms of reams of paper, rolls of filament, boxes of crayons) and then divide by 5. This will give you a number that represents the average daily use.

Table 10.1   How to Calculate Reorder Point

| Term | Definition | Example |
|---|---|---|
| **Average Daily Use** | Typical number of items used every day | 2 reams |
| **Lead Time** | Number of days for delivery | × 5 days |
| **Safety Stock** | The largest quantity used in one day | + 5 (unusually high use) |
| **Reorder Point** | The number of items left that indicates that it is time to reorder | 15 (reorder when you have 15 reams of paper left) |

Lead time may vary, but your vendor or supplier would be happy to estimate an anticipated delivery time on which you may base your calculations. Over time, however, you will be able to judge whether the vendor's estimate is accurate. If it is not, adjust your delivery time accordingly.

**Safety stock** can be determined by recalling a day when there was great demand, such as the week before the end of a school semester, an annual conference date, summer break. Use that unusually high demand count as your safety stock number.

Once you have established the reorder point, count out the number of items in inventory and place a card or paper on the supply stating, "It is time to reorder." Or an even better strategy would be to have the order form already completed and waiting at the actual inventory quantity that represents your reorder point so all you need to do is date the form and submit it to whomever is responsible for executing your purchases—a purchasing department or buyer. This trick will keep you from having to constantly count out the supplies to make sure you have enough on hand until an acquisition can be completed.

If you take the time to calculate the reorder point for several items when several items can be obtained from one vendor, do your best to reorder as many of these items at the same time, especially if you are paying shipping charges. You can do this by adjusting quantities of the lowest-cost item to conform to the reorder point of the highest total cost item. This will save you time by making only one order for several items while keeping expenditures evenly dispersed over time.

Remember, as with all processes, if your original estimates were not quite accurate, if the numbers you used were based on unusually high- or low-demand times of the year, you should be prepared to reevaluate your estimates and adjust your calculations after several months of observation. Refining all management practices is an ongoing project that you can do for yourself or your office team. It won't be long before you will need to spend very little time thinking about reordering and storing supplies, and you will have more time to spend on meeting the needs of your stakeholders.

## References

Muller, Max. *Essentials of Inventory Management*. AMACOM, 2003.
"Reorder point." Definition. BusinessDictionary.com. http://www.businessdictionary.com/definition/reorder-point.html
TradeGecko. "Reorder Point Formula—Know When to Reorder." *Inventory Management Software*, TradeGecko Blog, www.tradegecko.com/learning-center/reorder-point-formula-calculation

CHAPTER ELEVEN

# Change #7: Analyze Causes of Stressors and Take Precautions

If you are a manager with a staff, or if you manage yourself as the sole employee of the library, you are obligated to ensure the physical and emotional safety of anyone who enters that space, including yourself. What happens in the library, as both a public space and workplace, can have either a positive or negative impact on anyone who enters. Whatever requires troubleshooting, it's worth investing time to analyze stressors associated with the library and then do whatever is within your power to take positive actions or precautions. You will discover that the result of your efforts is improved customer service as well as employee job satisfaction.

## How Stressors Affect Efficiency

Employee demeanor or actions can broadcast the fact that there are stressors at play within an environment. Stressors can be caused by problems with management, the difficulty of tasks that library staff must complete, or the work roles for which each person is responsible. Stressors may be caused not only by the interpersonal dynamics of the people in the building, but also by the quality of the building itself and the surrounding area.

Any factor that creates stress in the library can, consequently, negatively impact the people the library was intended to serve. By eliminating as many of these factors as possible, you can create a welcoming atmosphere and convey the fact that the library is a positive and indispensable part of your community.

## Workplace Health and Safety

The objective of the National Institute for Occupational Safety and Health (NIOSH), as part of the U.S. Centers for Disease Control and Prevention, is to conduct research in the field of occupational safety and health. Stress in the workplace is one of the issues identified as a health risk for employees. NIOSH defines **job stress** as "the harmful physical and emotional responses that occur when the requirements of the job do not match the capabilities, resources, or needs of the worker." Stress is something that can permeate the whole environment, especially when the people suffering from stress subtly, or even at times overtly, convey negativity when interacting with others. It is problematic when the effects are not just reserved for coworkers but are made evident to the public as well.

Examples of overt demonstrations of stress can range from aggressive or angry attitudes to apathy. When individuals have been told that their positions are being phased out, when administrators are being put under scrutiny for their performance, or budget cuts result in eliminating positions and remaining staff are required to cover duties that do not match their education and skill level, the trickle-down effect causes people to lash out in anger or recoil into apathy. Being on the receiving end of this kind of behavior can be confusing and can cause the recipient to either "pay it forward" or fall into feelings of sadness or self-doubt. The negative effects can multiply from individuals to whole organizations, which then suffer increased absenteeism or poor morale.

While NIOSH states that short-lived or infrequent episodes of stress pose little risk, when stressful situations are ongoing, the body is at risk by being kept in a constant state of "fight or flight" response. This condition "increases the rate of wear and tear to biological systems." Ultimately, the person experiencing stress is not just unpleasant to be around but is becoming physically compromised. As fatigue or damage sets in, the body's ability to repair and defend itself is weakened. The outcome of being in a constant state of crisis is risk of injury or disease.

Some librarians, who have found themselves at odds with their supervisors when they once had excellent attendance records, may now find the need to take time off as they fall victim to colds, flu, or other infections; they brave days at work with back and neck pain or headaches. They even seem to be more accident prone: tripping over boxes or furniture, or even becoming involved in car accidents. Stress compromises people's immune systems, causes them to tense muscles to the point of severe pain, and can cause them to be distracted while engaging in everyday activities like walking or driving. Ultimately, when workers are ill,

*Change #7: Analyze Causes of Stressors and Take Precautions*

they are less able to perform their duties effectively. To prevent long-term health problems, it is essential to act.

Working to eliminate stress in the library or workplace is not to be confused with **stress management**. Stress management helps people cope with existing conditions by teaching them how to find balance between work and personal life, build a support network of friends and coworkers, or focus on maintaining a relaxed or positive outlook. Examples of stress management include meditation and mindfulness, seeking the advice of friends, commiserating, or venting. Management of environmental factors such as loud noise can be achieved with earplugs or headphones, excessive heat can be countered with fans or hydration, excessive cold can be lessened with warm coats and gloves. However, while these measures help alleviate the symptoms of stress, they're only temporary and don't serve to lessen the harm done to an individual's psyche or remove the causes of stress.

Improving stress- or pain-inducing tasks and environment is key to achieving a balance between work and self. When balance is achieved, the likelihood of successful interactions between staff and patrons increases, and positive energy results in increased customer satisfaction.

The Occupational Safety and Health Administration (OSHA), under the U.S. Department of Labor, was established "to assure safe and healthful working conditions for working men and women by setting and enforcing standards and by providing training, outreach, education." As a matter of health and safety, OSHA has identified four main factors that cause stress to most people:

1. Managers who lack proper management or communication skills,
2. Tasks that are poorly designed,
3. Work roles that cause uncertainty, and
4. Work environments that are toxic because of unsafe working conditions or strained interpersonal relationships.

The first stressor, management without adequate skills, leaves employees feeling undervalued or unappreciated. A newly assigned manager who fails to trust the judgment of a highly experienced employee can make the employee feel dejected. A disorganized administrator who leaves staff to field complaints of dissatisfied patrons can cause employees to leave the workday feeling demoralized. Failure to recognize employees' skill sets, or to give them opportunity to learn or to take on new responsibilities, can cause stress that dampens the drive for an otherwise motivated or productive member of the team.

How someone manages you, how you manage others, or even how you manage yourself can cause unnecessary stress. When there is a failure to communicate, understand, or address workplace issues in a timely manner, critical tasks can go unaccomplished. Likewise, failure to allow employees to make decisions, to participate in decision-making processes, or to have clearly established expectations causes difficulties in meeting deadlines or goals. Policies that cause work life to interfere with personal life can lead to resentment. When task management is not adequately dealt with by the manager, the whole environment reflects the effects by the attitudes and outlook of the employees.

The second stressor, poorly designed tasks, includes moving objects that are too heavy, not taking adequate rest breaks, working long hours, or engaging in hectic or routine tasks that have little inherent meaning. In some industries, especially in manufacturing, these can be stressors over which an employee may have very little control. In a library, however, these are issues that can be easily addressed by whomever is performing the tasks, but only if time and attention are taken to troubleshoot and remedy those tasks. Tasks that are easily redesigned can be check-in and shelving of materials, processing, and inventory, and attention can also be paid to workstation ergonomics.

The third stressor is uncertainty in work roles or tasks. When it is unclear what tasks should be handled, what specific expectations or procedures should be followed, or what the job actually entails (especially for occupations such as librarianship that are constantly evolving or being redefined in response to changes in technology or public demands), stress will ensue. With technology and digital resources becoming more prevalent, the lines between technology support and information specialists are blurred. Who troubleshoots hardware and who answers questions about software can be the same person, and that may leave the other wondering whether jobs are in danger. Confusion about how one can be productive, keep up with trends, take on new tasks without overstepping preestablished boundaries, bear the burden of finishing the work of others, or be held responsible for too many different tasks adds to feelings of uncertainty, which potentially results in unfinished critical tasks, time wasted duplicating efforts, or failure to meet expectations.

The fourth stressor, a toxic work environment, includes both the condition of the physical space and the condition of interpersonal relationships. Whether it is standing water under the foundation of the building that causes mosquitoes to breed and then the chemicals to be sprayed to stop the growth of larvae or mold that is growing in a storage room due to a leaky roof or air conditioning system, these environmental factors can be harmful to both the librarian and the patrons who spend time in the building. Likewise, coworkers holding grudges about politics, misunderstandings caused by gossip, or problems caused by breaches in confidentiality—all these situations result in lack of trust and an inability to work as a team. Both environmental and interpersonal factors make it difficult for workers to focus on achieving tasks. In either case, you, coworkers, volunteers, or even patrons who frequent the library will be physically unable to accomplish tasks in the library because of hazardous environmental conditions, or strained interactions between or among people.

Making the decision to deliberately bring about organizational changes such as improving work conditions, addressing workload expectations, or reducing or eliminating the stressors over which you have control will increase the probability of creating a more relaxed and positive atmosphere. You will discover that you, and others around you, are engaging in more positive interactions, are more capable of coping with negative or surprise events, and are achieving more successful outcomes in the library. Once this stage is reached, you will be able to engage in more exciting and intellectually challenging endeavors that exhilarate, not defeat, you. All of this can come to fruition simply because you are less physically and emotionally compromised.

## Process for Eliminating Stressors

As with all process management procedures, it is recommended that one problem be addressed at a time. For each stressor that has been identified, you can work toward eliminating them by following these basic steps:

- Start with identifying a problem. Discuss this with a team, a boss, or a volunteer. If you are alone, analyze and evaluate what you believe to be conditions that are a source of stress that may be causing health issues or dissatisfaction. This could be poor working conditions, unrealistic deadlines, lack of support from supervisors, inability to participate in decision making, or not having adequate authority or ability to perform your job duties.
- The next step is to design and implement interventions. Depending on what you have identified as the stressor, you can create strategies to address or eliminate it, prioritize the steps, and then implement the strategies from the most important to the least, in stages.
- End with evaluating the interventions for effectiveness. If the stressor has not been mitigated or eliminated, then you may not have identified the essential cause. You will need to reassess the situation and identify a different possible cause of the problem or redesign your interventions again.

It is essential to acknowledge that process management is a continuous and circular practice of identifying, strategizing, implementing, and evaluating as many times as necessary to discover to the heart of the problem and then get it fixed. If efforts to eliminate a stressor are unsuccessful at first, don't accept defeat. Go back and try again.

## Possible Targets for Intervention

### When Managers Lack Proper Management or Communication Skills

Sometimes managers place unrealistic expectations on their employees, or they fail to allow employees to utilize their skills, talents, or expertise by micromanaging their work. Psychology is beyond the scope of this book, but as this issue applies to space- and time-saving strategies, ask your manager to allow you to be, or invite your staff to be, involved in the problem-solving, troubleshooting process. A team that find themselves constantly working to meet last-minute deadlines may discover it is helpful to ask the most organized member to lead a team to create a shared calendar of regular events, contract renewal dates, holidays, and other predictable events, so unexpected events do not add undue pressure to the regular work process.

Deliberately exerting your experience and expertise to make improvements on processes that are problematic and enlisting the help of those who share tasks can help to reduce stress on yourself, coworkers, and even the manager who has thus far been unable to identify these issues. Taking the initiative to lead the change may be welcomed, as well as rewarding for you.

### When Tasks Are Poorly Designed

The essential question is how would you identify a poorly designed task? You will need to become self-aware of your behaviors while you perform tasks. Indicators of a poorly designed task in the library include:

- Feeling stiff or inflexible after retrieving books from a low desk or a deep or heavy book return
- Feeling sudden pulls or pinches when twisting and lifting books from low shelves or the bottom shelf of a book truck
- Experiencing fatigue or discomfort when shifting materials or engaging in a large weeding project
- Realizing that you are massaging your hands, arms, legs, neck, or back while performing any task
- Experiencing feelings of dissatisfaction with your employment, continually handling work on an emergent basis, or missing deadlines
- Dealing with malfunctioning equipment

*Change #7: Analyze Causes of Stressors and Take Precautions*

After identifying the tasks in need of improvement, begin to think about how you could make your job less physically demanding or more ergonomically efficient.

There are two kinds of ergonomic improvements to make for your physical safety:

1. **Engineering improvements:** changing the process, or the way of doing things, which may include replacing tools, products, or materials that you use to get your work completed; and
2. **Administrative improvements:** dissecting how or when a job is executed and then changing the timing or sharing the task with others.

*Engineering Improvements*

Engineering improvements require an objective analysis and dissection of processes (the way you do things) and deliberate action to minimize the required number of steps. This can be done by changing how tasks are executed, or by replacing tools, products, or materials for ones that will help to more effectively accomplish a task.

If you have trouble breaking down tasks on your own, ask a friend to observe you, or set up a device with a camera on a table or tripod. With a camera app on video or time-lapse function, you can document how you work with books at the return or shelves; how you pack or unpack boxes; or how you approach any other activity that may cause you pain or discomfort. If you are able, become self-aware of how you sit, stand, or work. Analyze the movement by asking yourself the following:

- Am I bending awkwardly? Does my bend include a twist? Am I facing shelves or tables head-on, or am I twisting sideways to handle materials?
- Can I look for changes to work practices by paying close attention to how the work is performed? Can I become more comfortable by changing positions or stretch during work periods?
- Can I implement recommendations established by NIOSH and OSHA when it comes to manual materials handling, as it applies to libraries?

*Manual Materials Handling*

The following information has been adapted from the NIOSH, and California OSHA service, 2007, and applied to library processes and activities. Manual materials handling, which is the majority of activity that a librarian will perform in the management of a collection, means that "workers' hands move individual containers or items by lifting, lowering, filling, emptying, or carrying them." Librarians regularly perform this set of activities when picking up, stacking, boxing, and unloading books daily.

Removing books from a book return; checking in and preparing books for return to the shelves; filling or emptying a box of materials for interlibrary loan; receiving and emptying boxes of copy paper, materials, supplies; receiving and emptying boxes of newly acquired books; weeding and boxing withdrawn materials; moving and emptying trash bins—all of these activities fall under the definition of manual materials handling.

### Why Does This Matter?

Moving materials improperly can lead to injuries when these activities are repeated daily (as with circulation activities) or occasionally and when excessive weight is involved (as with moving shipments of books, cases of copy paper, or tables and chairs for events). After sustaining injuries, it may either become impossible or take much longer to complete a task. It will cost money when you seek medical attention, and when you miss time from work while you recover.

Even if you haven't been injured yet, you may be expending too much energy by doing the task improperly. This also translates to increasing the length of time to complete the task. Over the course of your career, you will be placing yourself at risk for developing musculoskeletal disorders, which include damage to the back, shoulders, hands, wrists, muscles, tendons, ligaments, nerves, or blood vessels.

### Manual Materials Handling Recommendations

NIOSH has created manual materials handling guidelines to protect workers from unsafe lifting practices. As an individual, you can protect yourself from injury by following safer lifting guidelines when handling boxes of books, boxes of paper, containers of recycling, or large bins of supplies by:

- Stretching before you lift
- Testing boxes for stability and weight before you pick them up
- Using equipment, such as a dolly to move heavy or unstable loads (boxes that are not filled and where the contents can shift when they are moved) or heavy loads, or repack them into smaller containers
- Planning the lift by:
  - Wearing appropriate (closed-toe) shoes to avoid slip, trip, or fall
  - Wearing well-fitting gloves

*Change #7: Analyze Causes of Stressors and Take Precautions*

- Lifting only as much as you can safely handle by yourself
- Lifting within the power zone (the region of the body that is above the knees, below the shoulders, and close to the body)
- When lifting:
  - Get a secure grip
  - Use both hands
  - Use smooth motions
  - Keep the load close to the body
  - Use your legs to push up and lift (not the upper body or back)
  - Step from side to side or turn the entire body instead of twisting
  - Alternate heavy lifting with less physically demanding tasks
  - Take breaks

When carrying items such as stacks of books, stools, chairs, ladders, or boxes of materials, you can improve the carry by:

- Sliding, pushing or rolling items when appropriate
- Gradually increasing physical activities to meet physical demands
- Minimizing the distance items should be carried
- Utilizing a book truck, flatbed cart, or dolly to move items whenever possible
- Pushing instead of pulling
- Avoiding slopes, stairs, or other obstacles when carrying
- Making sure you have a clear view of your path when walking with heavy loads
- Carrying with two hands when possible
- When carrying with one hand, alternate hands
- Taking rest breaks

When using any kind of equipment for any task, make certain that you

- Receive adequate training on proper use of the equipment and on how to properly perform maintenance of the devices
- Provide instructions on the use of equipment with visual aids as a reminder to you, volunteers, or paid employees of the library
- Use powered, grounded (when electrical) equipment when possible
- Test carts or book trucks for stability prior to and after loading them with materials

- Choose vertical handles
- Choose equipment with wheels
- Push and pull with the entire body (not just arms and shoulders)

When moving materials manually, if you are alone and doing so is a challenge or a danger, be certain to utilize equipment such as a dolly or cart to move materials across a room; or to lift boxes from the floor to table height, utilize a pneumatic or scissor lift (Figure 11.1).

**Figure 11.1**  Scissor Lift

The cost for a scissor lift is about $1,500 for one with the ability to cart materials and lift 550 pounds to table height.

It may be surprising to you that even storing items on shelves can be improved by utilizing angled shelving, especially in a makerspace (Figure 11.2). If you make creative space available to students or young patrons and you need to constantly check supplies and replenish, you can help both others and yourself to improve access to containers with the right shelving in the right places for the right job.

## Handling Tasks Administratively

Changing when or the way you do things can also help to alleviate strenuous tasks. Alternating tasks such as shelving books with less strenuous ones such as desk work; mixing up tasks during the day instead of attempting marathon sessions; changing your schedule to do more labor-intensive work to a time of day when moving is a welcome change from sitting at a desk; taking time to move, stretch, and get comfortable before

**Figure 11.2**  Angled Shelves

continuing with or changing tasks are all administrative changes that can improve how tasks are completed.

You can determine if there are pressure points (places that are hard and irritating to the skin or sharp and ready to poke or scratch skin at your desk) at the circulation desk, at workstation tables, at the shelves.

Also, provide variety in jobs. You can do this by **job rotation**, which means rotating employees, or yourself, through different jobs, such as working at the circulation desk, then shelving materials. Or you could provide **job enlargement**, which is increasing variety by combining two or more jobs or adding tasks to a particular job. For example, while working the circulation desk you can also organize materials on a book truck for shelving later.

Both job rotation and enlargement rely on changing jobs and tasks so that different muscles or body parts are used; working postures such as sitting or standing change; and the amount of repetition, the pace of work, the amount of physical exertion, visual and mental demands, as well as environmental conditions change. For example, spending too much time processing materials or sitting in meetings, moving a heavy truck or boxes of books too quickly, working on a computer for too long, or sorting materials in a storage room with no air conditioning can take a toll on your physical well-being. However, stopping what you are doing to help a patron, which you might think is an interruption to your flow, is actually an opportune change in jobs because it gives you good reason to stand, walk, stretch, and change the line of vision!

### Sedentary Tasks in Librarianship

In addition to the physical part of managing a library, there is also sedentary work that must be done. Filling out reports, purchasing, cataloging, or answering e-mailed reference questions are all tasks that happen at the computer. OSHA recommends paying attention to potential problems with the wrists, back, and eyes when working at a desk and computer.

Intermittent stretching sessions are recommended to help alleviate potential carpal tunnel syndrome as well as lower back pain. Carpal tunnel syndrome occurs when repeated motions at the keyboard are performed without proper wrist placement. Take a break from the computer by stretching the arms, hands, and wrists to release tension; and when you return to the keyboard, keep your wrists above, not on, the wrist cushions of a mouse pad. Lower back pain can result from sitting with bad posture. When sitting too long in one position, your joints can become tight, hip flexors become shortened and tightened, and tight hip flexors can contribute to back pain. Standing, walking, and stretching intermittently will help to alleviate lower back pain.

Finally, eyestrain manifests with dry eye, headache, and sore neck. To alleviate the chances of eyestrain, you can take deliberate breaks to look away from the computer screen and increase the size of the fonts that you read. Table 11.1 at the end of this chapter lists NIOSH recommendations to improve safety and efficiency while handling materials in the library.

### Work Roles That Cause Uncertainty

Most librarians will agree that the duties and responsibilities of the profession are constantly changing, primarily because librarianship calls for constant response to the changing needs of the community. Whether the change is called for because of much-needed social services to the public or demands for school librarians to respond to constantly changing curriculum, there is a persistent need to learn and adapt. Public librarians may need to acquire an entirely new skill set that gives them the ability to respond to social needs and advances in technology spur the need for a school librarian to modify techniques or skills for delivery of instruction. For many people, changes in the type of information they need to deliver may cause uncertainty and stress—especially for those librarians who feel they have little or no time to acquire the new, necessary skills.

If mundane tasks are keeping you from spending time learning about new technologies, techniques, or advances in your profession, at the very least, you can work to control the amount of time you spend engaged in mundane tasks with the process management techniques that are available in this book. Controlling the time spent with the management of the library is the key to freeing up time for professional learning, self-study, and creating innovative ways of providing spaces that provide access to the resources that your community members demand.

The final stressor is a poor work environment. The environment can come from conditions either inside or outside of the building, and even include toxic interpersonal relationships that exist therein. Both these factors, one tangible and the other intangible, equally make it difficult for work to be accomplished.

The physical environment includes whether the library is poorly heated or not properly cooled; excessive noise or bad lighting; furniture or shelving in disrepair; materials cluttering the aisles or shelves. Likewise, the exterior of the library may contribute to severe health problems when there is standing water or hazardous materials outside or nearby. If you observe issues that seem to be dangerous and are uncertain about the dangers they pose, you should speak with your administrators about them. If you feel that your concerns will not be addressed, you may consider looking for the OSHA Log 300. This log will contain written complaints filed by former or current employees. You can also look for workers' compensation reports to determine the types of injuries employees have sustained while on the job.

Potentially as debilitating as environmental factors are **toxic interpersonal relationships**. This is what occurs when the stress levels have become unbearable in the workplace because of unaddressed stressors from tasks, job insecurity, undefined responsibilities, competition among employees, or other unmanaged conflicts. After addressing task management, there is a possibility that some of the relationship aspects will be mitigated. If you are in a situation that is irreparable, then it may be time to seek other employment. Remember, your health is at risk, and removing yourself from a bad situation may be the best, or only, option.

When you have done all that you can to improve your activities and have taken all possible measures to implement injury prevention programs, not only will you have increased efficiency and productivity in the library, you also will have taken significant steps toward reducing the costs of injuries, illnesses, and possible fatalities that affect not just individuals but communities as well.

**Table 11.1   NIOSH Recommendations to Improve Safety and Efficiency**

- Have deliveries placed at the workstation where materials will be handled, or move the material handling workstation near to the place of delivery
- Move smaller quantities of books or lighter boxes at first, but then gradually increase quantities or weight over time
- Avoid lifting and lowering heavy containers from or to the floor
- Have deliveries of heavy materials placed directly on tables or shelving
- For unstable loads (containers that are heavy or not full)
  - Label the container "unstable" as a reminder
  - Reduce the weight by putting fewer or smaller, or lighter weight items in the container
  - Repack so they are stable
  - Have multiple people share the effort when moving unstable containers
- Clear spaces to improve access to materials being handled

*Source: Applications Manual for the Revised NIOSH Lifting Equation*, which can be found on the NIOSH website (http://www.cdc.gov/niosh/docs/94-110/).

## References

"About OSHA." Occupational Safety and Health Administration. United States Department of Labor. https://www.osha.gov/about.html

Chang, Althea. "6 Serious Office Health Risks." TheStreet, May 18, 2010. https://www.thestreet.com/story/12806063/1/6-serious-office-health-risks.html

"Computer Vision Syndrome." American Optometric Association. https://www.aoa.org/patients-and-public/caring-for-your-vision/protecting-your-vision/computer-vision-syndrome

"Injury and Illness Prevention Programs: White Paper," Jan. 2012. Occupational Safety and Health Administration. https://www.osha.gov/dsg/InjuryIllnessPreventionProgramsWhitePaper.html

"STRESS . . . At Work." National Institute for Occupational Safety and Health/Centers for Disease Control and Prevention. https://www.cdc.gov/niosh/docs/99-101/default.html

"Understanding the Effect of Pain and How the Human Body Responds." *Nursing Times*, Feb. 26, 2018. https://www.nursingtimes.net/clinical-archive/pain-management/understanding-the-effect-of-pain-and-how-the-human-body-responds/7023422.article

CHAPTER TWELVE

# Change #8: Weed and Clear the Library Space

When you have the feeling that it is time to make big changes to the library space, even when you aren't exactly sure what changes need to be made, you can prepare to assess the library for its potential for change by focusing your efforts on removing irrelevant, obsolete, or outdated materials, supplies, furniture, or fixtures. Clearing out the library space of items that are no longer of use is the best way to get a clearer vision of the possibilities for improving the library to create the space and provide the service that your community values and demands.

## Getting Started with Decluttering

When you're working with a space that is older, cluttered, and seems to have not been cleaned out since the doors first opened "back in the day," it can be a bit overwhelming and difficult to know where to start. First, ask yourself the following questions:

- What objects have not been used in the past two years?
- What keeps the space from functioning as you wish it would?
- Is valuable storage space being wasted by warehousing obsolete materials or technology?
- Are you keeping things in storage for one person who doesn't value it enough to keep it in their own custody?
- What is in the space for "just in case"?
- Is this item dangerous to use?

When you begin clearing and removing undesirable things, the first to go should be items that are a potential hazard, especially when they are in the main library space. Soiled, torn, or ready-to-fall-apart chairs, tables, or shelves must be removed immediately. If any unsuspecting individual attempts to use it, and it is potentially dangerous, it must go, no questions asked, right now! Also, if your space has too many shelves or they are so tall that they obstruct views, they should be moved or removed and replaced with shelves that make it possible for you to monitor the room. Obstructed views are a possible danger to you and anyone who visits the library.

The next location to remove items from is in your storage space. Storage closets are meant to hold supplies and materials that are actively accessed regularly. When storage is filled permanently with unused, obsolete, or broken video cameras, slide projectors, telephones, boom boxes, cassette players, overhead projectors, or even old computer monitors, take measures to remove them. If the removal depends on someone from another department to take the initiative or to create documentation for removal, get the paperwork started by filling out serial numbers, inventory control numbers, or whatever tedious detail work needs to be recorded for whomever is responsible for those items. If any equipment is broken and has not yet been removed for repair, it is most likely not needed and should be included in the list for removal, as well. In schools, where there is a teacher who insists that a piece of equipment will be needed one day, remove it from the inventory and put it in their custody. If it's used by another department, transfer it to their location. If that piece of equipment is important to them, they will be willing to store it themselves and perhaps use it even more. As the old saying goes, "out of sight, out of mind."

Finally, when you store supplies and oddities "just in case," if you haven't used it in the past year, or if you have no definite plans for using it within the next 3 months, get rid of it or put it out in a makerspace to be used by creative minds who are in need of unusual things to explore.

For all the things that are collecting dust, being kept for a "one-time, maybe, possibly" event, there may be extremely useful or even valuable things, hidden out of sight, behind all the junk. The longer the junk remains, the greater the risk that hidden treasures fall into obsolescence as well. Also, equipment and materials that are being kept locked up because they might be destroyed if mishandled were not purchased to be permanently stored away for their own protection. You must resist the urge to preserve materials or equipment for fear of damage. Be prepared to teach the users how to properly handle the item, but then let it go. It must be allowed to circulate because it was purchased to be used.

Change #8: Weed and Clear the Library Space

Before you begin removing furniture and equipment from the premises, be sure to consult with your municipality's or school district's property management office before you throw it out or physically take it away. You must follow proper procedures or protocol for asset removal or transfer. Then, once the library is properly cleared of unnecessary objects, you may observe the cleared space that remains. With the emptiness in plain sight, you can get a better vision of a new arrangement.

## Weeding the Collection

As part of your removal of unwanted or unnecessary furniture and equipment, you can now work to decrease the number of books in your collection. Routine weeding of the library collection helps to keep the materials current and relevant. When you discover damaged materials, incomplete sets, or materials that have been superseded with newer, more current materials, weed these items right away. This will save you the time and effort of working around useless books, and it will save your patrons time from having to search for what they want from among undesirable materials. Once you have the collection left with only the highest-quality resources, you will be in a position for decision making about the space.

### Degrees of Weeding

Routine weeding is a benefit for not just librarians but patrons as well. Continuous Review Evaluation Weeding (CREW) helps you to work on the regular maintenance of the collection. With this method, whenever you happen to find a book or other material during the usual course of business, you decide its fate: withdraw it because it doesn't meet standards or keep it because it is still useful. You can even utilize the MUSTY (MUSTI) rule. When you happen to locate a book that is misleading, ugly, superseded, trivial, or irrelevant to the collection, you should immediately weed it.

But even with regular attention to weeding, there are times when it is beneficial to dig deeper into the collection. When faced with the prospect of rearranging, reorganizing, or even renovating, this is the precise occasion to take greater measures for a more aggressive weeding project. But before you begin the project, find out or decide what will be the final destination of the withdrawn materials. If the materials will be recycled, you may not need to do anything more than withdraw them from the library management system and then box them for delivery to a recycling service. You may need to establish a location to prepare materials for withdrawal. The receiving, processing, repair station may be a good option for weeding.

You'll need a weeding station for several reasons. First, if you are utilizing the municipal recycling and waste management services, you may need to separate or remove the cover from the contents. The weeding station, like the processing station, should be located out of sight of the general public. The reason for this is that witnessing a wholesale weeding process can be startling to the untrained eye, especially when the librarian is seen slicing the binding and tearing the contents out of lots of books!

If the books will be donated or sold to recuperate funds, in addition to the weeding station, there should be a prepared storage space. The weeding station should have property stamp removal tools (permanent markers, boxes, scissors, packing tape, a "withdrawn" stamp, if you are required to stamp withdrawals), as well as a laptop or computer to scan barcodes to remove them from the collection's database.

When you weed, approach the task with a hardened heart. Now is not the time to be sentimental about pristine and outdated copies of books that nobody has ever read—even if it was your childhood favorite. Times change and so have the people and their preferences for reading. The more you overthink the removal of these books or waste time trying to relocate them so you can see if you can get some circulation out of them, the longer the process of weeding will take. When you weed underutilized materials, you may even decide to eliminate the over-circulated books as well. You can replace worn books with new copies in the future.

You can further expedite a thorough weeding project by printing a list of books that fit predetermined criteria. Use your library management system to generate a report of materials to be weeded based on low circulation, such as "less than three circulations in the past three years," and/or copyright dates greater than 8 years old. If the list looks too long, don't panic. It's best to remove old, unused copies all at once, so you don't need to repeat the whole process too soon. Using a threshold of 8 years old gives you 2 years before nonfiction materials are considered outdated when the copyright date is 10 years old. Generate a hard copy list so you, or a volunteer, can use it to keep track of what you pull from the shelves. With a cart, list, and pencil in hand, beginning with the 000s and continuing through the 900s, pull books reserving judgement as to the value. If a decision needs to be made, err on the side of the book has little to no value remaining. It has already been labeled as outdated and uncirculated by your list, so if it is necessary, remind yourself that if it hasn't been checked out in the

Change #8: Weed and Clear the Library Space

past three years, chances are that it won't be missed anytime soon. As you come across the over-circulated books, place those on your cart for removal too, and do not waste time second-guessing yourself.

Are there instances when you would want to keep certain outdated materials? The answer is yes, especially if the library:

- is an archive
- holds out-of-print books that are of special interest to the community
- has books that are of historical value to the community
- is a special library and the book is a foundational text

If your library and its contents do not meet these criteria, then realize the collection is meant to serve the current needs of the public. You will serve your patrons well to keep it streamlined, current, and fresh. If you have a significant collection of items of historical value to your community, consider creating a separate, archival library for noncirculating, curated materials. The archival library can simply be a room with a few shelves and a table for viewing books, documents, or historic records for the community. You may also consider donating these materials to the local museum.

## Special Considerations for School Libraries

When it comes to weeding a school library, because of the ownership that the community has in the space and its contents, emotions can run high. If the librarian is new to the campus and the existing parent volunteers, teachers, or students witness an aggressive weeding effort that is spearheaded for a fresh start, they may feel inclined to "report this to the principal!" "Certainly this is unacceptable behavior, and the librarian has no clue of what they are doing!" Even with more experienced librarians, if they are seen piling up books on the tables or marking out property stamps, they might be accused of "going crazy" because they are removing "everything" from the shelves. If withdrawn books need to be pulled apart for recycling, you can be certain that a taxpayer will experience nothing but horror from the sight of a librarian slicing the binding and removing the contents from a book. "What a waste of taxpayer dollars!" A concerned teacher may even feel the need to confront the librarian, making for a most difficult conversation about "value" and "importance" and "what is best for the children."

If you have never heard these comments or arguments, you have never properly weeded a library. If you have, you know that debates or discussions such as these rarely result in a reformed view of weeding for the person who objects to the process. Even if you are the most eloquent and persuasive of speakers, there will still be hurt feelings when you respectfully decline to allow the teacher to rescue the old books from their weeding fate. You can ask someone, "If the book isn't good enough to be in the library, why would it be good enough for a classroom?" The individual may pretend to understand, but in reality, there will be no meeting of the minds. People will insist that someone can use that old book for something. But unless the art teacher is prepared to deconstruct the book to use it as materials for a project right now, books that are not removed from the premises almost invariably end up back in the library, in the hands of a concerned citizen who "found this book and thought I should bring it back to you."

For all these reasons, it is best to weed when you are alone or with the help of an assistant or volunteer who understands the process and why it needs to happen. You should also weed in a discreet manner. Taking all materials to a back room for withdrawal procedures, boxing them, and storing them in a closet until they are picked up for disposal is the best way to conduct a large weeding project. By weeding at a designated space that is out of sight, and sending the books off for proper disposal according to your district, city, county, or state policy, you will be saving time during the weeding process. After it is complete, a positive relationship with your stakeholders will be preserved.

In any library with a well-maintained collection, you will spend less time shelving books (eliminating the need to place desirable books among a collection of undesirable books), and your patrons will spend less time searching for desirable books from among a collection of irrelevant or dated materials, or incomplete series.

Once you have the library collection down to the most desirable of materials, you can stand back and evaluate the space. Does it appear that some shelves are no longer needed? Is there a possibility of rearranging the materials based on what is most popular? Are you now able to adjust the focus on the types of materials or services that your community demands? With a streamlined collection, the vision may become clearer to you now. You might now have reimagined the space, and now you are prepared to make changes.

## References

"Collection Maintenance and Weeding." American Library Association, Dec. 25, 2017. www.ala.org/tools/challengesupport/selectionpolicytoolkit/weeding

Dilevko, Juris, and Lisa Gottlieb. "Weed to Achieve: A Fundamental Part of the Public Library Mission?" *Library Collections, Acquisitions, and Technical Services*, vol. 27, no. 1, 2003, pp. 73–96., doi:10.1016/s1464-9055(02)00308-1

Larson, Jeanette. "CREW: A Weeding Manual for Modern Libraries." Texas State Library and Archives Commission, Austin, 2008. www.tsl.texas.gov/ld/pubs/crew/index.html

CHAPTER THIRTEEN

# Change #9: Reconfigure the Library Space

After you have taken measures to remove furniture, fixtures, books, and equipment that are no longer of service to you or your community, now's the time to examine the library space that's clear of clutter and full of possibilities.

The goal for a library reconfiguration is to strike a balance between the shelf space and the empty space so you can both facilitate ease of access to materials and create places for both groups and individuals to meet and enjoy. Where you locate and how you arrange materials, shelves, furniture, and fixtures is not something that should be done strictly for aesthetics. Location of key features such as the circulation desk, shelves, and seating also must provide ease of service and facilitate patron needs.

When providing library service feels difficult or more complicated than it should be, it becomes evident that the library may have been built to showcase architectural features, with little regard for library operations. Decisions made for placement of shelves, tables, and other gathering spaces without foresight can cause excessive amounts of time and energy to be spent managing circulation and preparing for programming. However, when a library is arranged with purpose, it can result in time and energy savings for those who manage the holdings and increase the likelihood that library attendees will enjoy the facility as well.

Before you decide on any new rearrangement, it pays to conduct some research before moving heavy furniture and shelves. Spending some time with a discovery process may save you from making some serious time- and labor-wasting mistakes.

## Step One: Locate and Refer to "Blueprints"

When you're ready to reconfigure the library space, your first step should be to locate what was once known as the **blueprints** or, more currently, the **sheets** or **construction drawings**.

Once you have located construction drawings, after you have completed the process of removing hazardous furniture and fixtures, weeding and removing outdated, damaged, and obsolete books and equipment as discussed in Chapter 12, you will be prepared to decide how to rearrange, or reconfigure, shelves and tables. Any of the construction plans will facilitate a reconfiguration strategy, but ideally, the electrical plan will give you valuable information such as the exact size of the library facility and the location of electrical wires within and outlets on the walls. This will help you gain a realistic picture of the changes you'll be able to make, and you'll be prepared to discuss with facilities managers whether these changes are safe, logical, or financially possible in the immediate future.

Library construction plans will help you to make drawings of the space and the contents such as furniture and shelves. You can draw the contents of the library to scale on paper and arrange and rearrange them easily. Moving small pieces of paper that represent shelves, tables, computer stations may help you discover that minor changes or adjustments can be enough to vastly improve the functionality of the space. However, as you begin to reconfigure, you might realize that additions of carts or cabinets, or changes in seating, shelving, or work surfaces, may be helpful to update and accommodate patron demands. You may also discover that slight changes in the location of seating or computers will require an addition of electrical outlets or more wireless access points. Changes that seemed minor at first blush may end up being more labor and materials intensive than you originally anticipated. Now, the amount of funds that are available will have bearing on the changes you will ultimately be able to make. If this is the situation you are now facing, you may need to build a case to convince the keepers of funds that allocating a portion of it to the library renovation is in order.

## Step Two: Build a Case for Change

If you need to provide thoroughly researched evidence for making changes, especially if you need permission from an administrator, a board of trustees, or a facilities manager, you can gather support for your proposal by documenting observations of how people have been using the library facility. You could describe what measures your patrons have had to take to make the space work for them. Add photos of what patrons have done to make the space usable or a compilation of comments, concerns, or complaints to use as evidence or to bring attention to the need for improvements to the library.

For example, you may have noticed that students who enter your library to study before school or between classes end up sitting on the floor next to a limited number of electrical outlets to recharge their phones or laptop computers. They may even move heavy furniture together or out of the way so they can work in small groups for projects or to study for an exam. Maybe you've even seen individuals scowling and shushing those collaborative groups, who clearly need a gathering place but are now infringing on the rights of the silent readers or researchers. It wouldn't be difficult to take a quick photo of either the individuals or groups as they are working and adjusting, or the aftermath with the moved furniture. Photos, along with short narratives of what transpired, can serve as evidence for the need for modifications to be made.

Your administration may then ask that you take further steps by creating a formal survey. Surveys shouldn't be taken lightly. If they are taken frequently and there is no modification, your respondents will learn to stop wasting their time voicing their opinions. So, if you are given permission to create a survey, verify that some sort of action will follow, and then, to respect your respondents' time, try to be as concise as possible.

### Constructing a Survey

Using a combination of structured and open-ended questions will help you to determine your patrons' priorities for library service. Table 13.1 shows some examples of survey questions that can be used to determine patron wants or needs. Begin with demographics, organized by the age range that defines your toddler, child, teen, young adult, adult, or retired adult markets—all of these groups may have different needs or expectations. Then look for occupation information to determine the type of services the respondent may typically be interested in. Even though toddlers will not be responding for themselves, you may wish to acknowledge them as a service group so that parents feel that their response on behalf of their babies' needs are important. Children to seniors and retirees can express, with assistance or for themselves, which programs will enrich and improve their quality of life.

Asking for a response to the frequency of library visits will help to determine whether this respondent is an occasional or heavy user of library service and will help you to weigh how well informed the responses are. Also,

Table 13.1  Patron Survey of Library Service

| | | |
|---|---|---|
| Structured: Demographic | Age | 0–4 |
| | | 5–10 |
| | | 11–18 |
| | | 19–23 |
| | | 24–50 |
| | | 51+ |
| | Select one of the following that best describes your current occupation. | Preschool |
| | | Student: elementary, secondary, postsecondary |
| | | Seeking employment |
| | | Part-time employed |
| | | Full-time employed |
| | | Homemaker/Primary caregiver |
| | | Retired |
| Structured: Usage about any library | How often do you visit any library, including this library, per month? | 0–1 |
| | | 2–4 |
| | | 5 or more times |
| | Which services do you look for at any library? Number in order of priority, 1 being most important, 10 least important. | Check out books |
| | | Reference (help from the librarian) |
| | | Library space for study or reading independently |
| | | Library space for gathering with groups |
| | | Computers and Wi-Fi access |
| | | Databases (including articles, journals, streaming media, e-books, e-audiobooks, e-video) |
| | | Library programs and events (book club, makerspace, story time, information fairs, adult and community education, etc.) |

(continued)

Change #9: Reconfigure the Library Space

**Table 13.1** (*continued*)

| | | |
|---|---|---|
| Structured: Usage about this library | Which library services do you use at this library? Check if same as above, or number in order of priority, 1 being most important, 10 least important if you use services differently at this library | Check out books |
| | | Reference (help from the librarian) |
| | | Library space for study or reading independently |
| | | Library space for gathering with groups |
| | | Computers and Wi-Fi access |
| | | Databases (including articles, journals, streaming media, e-books, e-audiobooks, e-video) |
| | | Library programs and events (book club, makerspace, story time, information fairs, adult and community education, etc.) |
| | Time of day you most often visit this library: check all that apply. | Weekdays a.m. |
| | | Weekdays p.m. |
| | | Weekends a.m. |
| | | Weekends p.m. |
| Unstructured/ Open-ended questions | What do you like most about this library? | |
| | What do you like least about this library? | |
| | What would you change about this library? | |
| | Are there any comments or suggestions that you could provide to help us better understand your library needs? | |

the time of day and day of the week that the library is frequented will provide insight into the best times to offer service so that it will be utilized.

With unbiased, structured, non-leading questions posed first, the respondents will be better prepared and informed to answer more open-ended opinion questions at the end. You may find valuable information or ideas in responses to questions such as "what do you like least," "what do you like most," and "what would you change about the library?"

Before you consider creating a school library survey, you will need to get permission from administration or a board of directors, especially if it is going out to the public, and you may even need to get approval to survey students. If you can design a survey instrument, you may be able to minimize the number of questions if your population is somewhat homogeneous.

Your population or demographic question can simply be addressed by groups such as students, teachers, parents, administration, or community members. You can ask how often they visit the library outside of scheduled class visits, and then ask any other relevant question for which you need answers. Keep your questions simple and readable for your youngest readers to understand, and administer the same survey to all participants to simplify the data analysis.

If you have any specific questions you would like to ask, such as, "Would you participate in or refer a friend to . . . (specify a public service)," be sure to add them. After examining the results of the survey, you'll have a better understanding of who your patrons are, what they value in a library, and when they need access.

## Step 3: Refine Your Plans with Patron Needs in Mind

Once you've documented the wants and needs of the patrons in the library, you'll want to refine your reconfiguration plans. When you do, you should adhere to some key rules or precepts of placement of key services or materials in a space. These precepts that are being adapted for use in a library are based on marketing and warehousing fundamentals. The first group of precepts pertain to users of library space.

For users of library pace:

- Individuals may want quiet space to work in both private and public space. Some people enjoy solitary space to concentrate or study, and others seek to work among people so they don't feel isolated.
- Groups also may need private and public space for study and collaboration, but also for socializing and gathering.

Placement of special features of space can be prioritized by:

- Determining what is the greatest priority to the community, then addressing that need first and placing it in the most ideal or prominent space in the library

- Locating public gathering places at the main entry
- Locating private collaborative workspace near the front of the library but in closed spaces so as not to disturb those in quiet gathering space
- Placing quiet, individual spaces around the perimeter of the library, in corridors along the stacks, in the back of the library, or even among the stacks
- Storing low-circulating items toward the back of the large space
- Storing high-circulating items toward the front of the large space, and close to the circulation desk

School libraries will ideally accommodate:

- One or two whole group instructional spaces
- An area for small group instruction
- Space for individuals to work

Adhering to these fundamental rules when you rearrange the library space will help increase your ability to meet the needs of your stakeholders while minimizing the workload for you, staff, or volunteers.

### Aligning Precepts with Patron Needs

Now that you have identified the needs of your patrons from observation or a survey, organize the needs in order of importance and then align the precepts to those needs. As an example for a public library, if the majority of your community expresses the need to enter the library quickly to pick up a book on hold or browse the newest releases, your priority will be to place a holds shelf and new release shelf that is large enough to accommodate the demand, and close enough to the circulation desk so that people can access, check out, and be on their way. If the second-greatest priority is computer and Wi-Fi access, a bank of computers and comfortable seating for use with personal devices should be nearby. As the priorities fall toward the lower end of the scale, the spaces that accommodate each of the needs will fall toward the back or the perimeter of the space.

You should also analyze the circulation statistics of the library resources. What is most popular? What do people most often want, request, or need? For some libraries, it may be fiction books that circulate more than nonfiction. Graphic novels or manga may be a popular genre as well. Some people will guess that certain materials are more important, but the proof is in the statistics. Whatever you discover to be the case, that section should be closer to the front door and the rest can work around whatever is most popular.

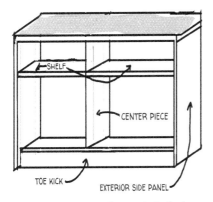

**Figure 13.1**   Bookcase Labeled

## Step 4: Plan the Move

Reconfiguring the library space can be planned with a series of photos, drawings, or to-scale models before making the effort to move vast quantities of heavy books, shelves, and furniture. With aggressively weeded shelves, you can determine if you can shift the collection so you can remove shelves that have no books on them at all. When there are empty shelves, you can disassemble them and remove or relocate them to a better place or enlist the assistance of professional movers who may be able to move the shelves intact. The other shelves with books still on them should be approximately 30 to 33 percent full, and will now be easier for a team of people to make proximal changes to a new location.

If the shelves were originally placed in long continuous aisles, with far more than three cases with no breaks in between, now will be a good time to separate or shorten the length. Providing walking space between shelves eliminates the need, and time spent, to travel all the way down an endless aisle to the end to get to the next aisle that runs parallel. Most shelves that are not custom built can be easily disassembled or separated. See Figure 13.1, which diagrams and labels the parts of a case of shelves.

If removing a portion of the bookcase leaves the center piece, or middle support panels, with exposed drill holes, use the recently exterior, or end panel, to replace the middle support panel to restore the case to a finished look. If you have more exposed center pieces than you have exterior pieces, consider hiring a carpenter to add molding to conceal the exposed holes, or if you know the vendor that supplied the shelves originally, inquire if they have replacement exterior pieces available for your shelves.

### Shifting Contents of the Shelves

Moving the contents of one shelf to another shelf relatively nearby is called **shifting**. This is done to adjust for increases or decreases in the number of books that fit or no longer fit on a single shelf. You can shift the shelves to improve access to books, or to facilitate locating books by beginning a class or group of books on a top shelf, or to fit an entire section of books onto a single case. When making small adjustments like this, shifting can be a relatively easy task with little planning necessary.

But to move an entire section of books to improve the flow, organization, or location in a building, it is best to be ready with an organized plan.

## Reasons to Relocate Entire Collections or Sections of Books

You may have decided that moving books to another location across the room, or to another room within the building, has become necessary. For example, if the demand for fiction titles has surpassed the demand for nonfiction, moving your fiction books to the front of the library and nonfiction toward the back would make sense. Similarly, if digital resources are a preferred source in research for your patrons, you may conclude that your former reference section may serve people better as a comfortable area to access free Wi-Fi. If you still have VHS, DVDs, and CDs on your shelves in the front of the library and you notice that circulation is virtually nonexistent with increased use of streaming media, maybe that area could be used to display best sellers, new acquisitions, or graphic novels. Or if you are in a rural area, with bad connectivity, DVDs and CDs may be your community's lifeline for entertainment. Those items need to be in the front. Why send people deep into the library to get high-demand items when moving them to a prime location or the best shelf in the library would serve them better? Not only will this help people to get what they want quickly, it will also save you time when returning them to the shelves.

Without a plan, the process of relocating whole collections of materials can become overwhelming, and the effect can become quite explosive. Engineers regularly plan the relocation of large pallets of materials in warehouses to ensure that inventory in greatest demand is kept to the front of a warehouse with the goal of reducing time spent accessing and restocking. **Reslotting** is the name given to the efficiently executed movement of materials from one location to another to ensure that high-demand items are placed in **prime locations** or the best shelves, such as those in the front of the warehouse (or in our case, the library), so access and replacement are quick and easy. In the library, accessing and returning books to the shelves will be most efficient when the distance among the front door, the most popular materials, and the circulation desk is as close as possible. For our purposes, we can call the most proximal area to the front of the library or circulation desk our prime location or our best shelf in the library. This is the area where we want our most popular collection to begin or the bookcase we want our highest-demand books to be shelved. Lower-demand items can be kept to the back of the library because they may be accessed less frequently, but still need to be readily available.

In a warehouse, reslotting is a constant process and essential to keep customer satisfaction high. A plan to do this is always in place. Similarly, in a library, reslotting can be utilized regularly when holiday-themed books are displayed in a prominent location, or newly acquired books are placed on a special shelf for access. As the holiday and the newness pass, the materials are moved out for the next celebration or new batch of releases. Occasionally, however, a librarian may find a time when large-scale moves are in order. This decision may depend on the fact that demand for certain types of media or material has changed over time, or the needs of patrons have evolved with the availability of new types of resources and tools to access them. In order to deliver the materials and services in demand, a better arrangement in the space is necessary to improve access. Because it isn't every day that you decide a large-scale move is necessary, the practice of reslotting is optimal to bring about greater function and access of the library and its resources to improve the daily movement of materials.

Reslotting is easier to execute than it is to explain. But chances are you have already reslotted materials on a small scale. For example, you may have a charging cart of laptop computers and have already labeled both the laptops and the slots with numbers or letters so the equipment can be placed in its own charging port. (You would do this so you could quickly identify which laptop is missing if the designated slot is open.) Chances are that after a whole group finishes using the laptops, when returned to the cart, they are placed without regard for the numbering system. When you go to fix the misplaced laptops, you can do one of two things:

1. You can remove all the laptops and place them on the floor, then proceed to pick up and replace them in the correct slot, or
2. You can remove a laptop and directly place it in the correct slot. If you discover there is already a laptop in that slot, you can simultaneously remove the second misplaced laptop with your second hand before you replace the correct laptop in its designated slot.

The process is either "remove, place, pick up, replace" from slot to floor then from floor to slot, or it is "remove and replace" from slot to slot.

If you are only moving one or two items, 4 steps versus 2 steps is somewhat inconsequential. But now, imagine that you have 30 laptops in the cart. If you use the first option, you are executing 4 steps, 30 times. This is 120 steps to restore the laptops to their proper location. However, if you use the second option, you only need to perform 2 steps, 30 times, or 60 steps to accomplish the same result.

Now let's apply the laptop example to the movement of entire cases of books. The books are already labeled with call numbers. When rearranging collections, you can mark the shelves with labels that indicate where

Change #9: Reconfigure the Library Space

you want the materials to belong. The goal is to get the groups of books into the correct "slot" on the shelves in as few steps as possible: remove and replace. To do this similarly to the "laptops in the cart" example, some preplanning is necessary. The time spent preplanning, however, will save you lots of physical labor, so it is well worth the investment.

### Plan to Reconfigure a Library

The entire planning process to reconfigure a library can be done by performing the following steps:

1. Create a working plan-o-gram.
2. Create two labels for the contents of each shelf.
3. Gather one of the labels from each shelf, keeping them in shelf order.
4. Make changes to the shelves (if necessary).
5. Redistribute the collected labels to the books' new destination location.
6. Finalize the plan-o-gram.
7. Move materials using the two-cart system.
8. Remember to employ safe materials handling practices as outlined in Chapter 11.

### Create a Plan-O-Gram

A **plan-o-gram** is a diagram that illustrates where you want the materials to be located after you have reconfigured the space. It is to be referred to frequently during the move to ensure that all materials are being relocated to the new, intended destination. The initial plan-o-gram that you create is basically a working copy of a map of where you want the shelves, materials, and workspaces to be at the end of the reconfiguring project. But since we are amateur planners, be flexible and prepared to adjust when the reality of the space and the vision need to be reconciled.

### Label the Contents of the Shelves

To prepare for slotting, before you move any shelves, you should mark the contents of the shelves with a big, obvious label so it can be seen from a distance, and have an equally big and obvious label to mark where you want the materials to go. To do this, use two reams of copy paper or card stock in different colors. White and yellow paper would work well. With this paper, you can create two large labels, one in white and one in yellow, with identical information. They can be handwritten with thick permanent marker, to clearly identify the books that are on the shelves.

The labels should indicate the range of books that are located on each shelf. For example, the shelves of fiction books would be labeled Fic A, if all your fiction A books fit on one shelf. Sections or Dewey classes of books that take up more than one shelf should have labels that indicate the call number of the first and last book on that shelf. For example, 398.2 Aar–398.2 DeP; 398.2 Eli–398.2 Ham, and so on.

After you have made two labels for each shelf in two different colors, duplicating the call number information on both the white sheet of paper and the yellow sheet of paper, make sure you have labeled every shelf in the library whose contents you intend to move. When you have finished creating labels for the entire library, scan the room to verify that each shelf has two labels with identical information, in two different colors.

### *Gather One of the Labels from Each Shelf, Keeping Them in Shelf Order*

When you've finished creating labels, collect only the yellow labels from all the shelves, keeping them in Dewey order. Let the white label remain with the books. The white label will stay with the books as they wait on the shelf, travel on the cart, and are then placed where they ultimately belong: from the origin shelf, to the travel cart, to the destination shelf. But before you begin moving books, now is the time to reconfigure the shelves if this is part of your plan.

## Reconfiguring the Shelves

After you've fully planned the move with labels and a plan-o-gram that illustrate what your vision is for the future location of materials and shelves, it is time to move the shelves where you ultimately want them to be. It would be wise to tape the white labels to a book or directly on the shelf before allowing the shelves to be physically moved to make sure the labels don't fall off.

Ideally, your plan will require only removing unwanted shelves, shifting cases by a few feet, or adjusting the angle or direction of the stacks. But no matter how minor or major the adjustments, moving whole stacks that still hold even small numbers of books any distance will require that you enlist the help of qualified movers. With a copy of the plan-o-gram in hand, at your direction, the movers will be able to clearly see and understand your vision of where the shelves should be relocated. Remember, you need to protect yourself from injury, so moving library shelves is never a task to be done alone.

### Redistribute the Shelf Labels

Once the shelves are in their new location, you can then distribute the yellow labels where you want the materials to be at the end of your reconfiguration project. Before you make the final placement of the yellow labels, you can easily "play around" with the destination location of the books simply by shifting and rearranging the labeled sheets of paper. Do this until you feel satisfied that the books will be placed in a location that makes sense, provides easy access, and flows logically. Books should flow from top to bottom shelf, left to right across cases, and in a continuous direction so that gaps and jumps in the sequences, or order, are minimized.

As you work with the paper labels, you'll soon appreciate that the time that it took to create labels for the materials was time well spent. As you move and adjust the labels, remember that you would have otherwise been shifting and lifting entire shelves of books!

### Finalize the Plan-O-Gram

When the yellow labels are in place, and you are satisfied with the new location of the books, you may need to relabel the plan-o-gram, especially if you made significant changes while working with the yellow labels. Be certain that any changes in shelf location are reflected in the plan-o-gram because the original, theoretical plan, versus the now actual location, may be different after unforeseen problems are resolved, or unexpected opportunities for improvements are taken.

Referring to our laptop cart example, all the above steps would have occurred initially, when the laptops and slots were labeled. You also could have created a diagram of the labeled cart to serve as directions so users of the laptops would understand where everything belongs. Now you are about to employ the process that gets the laptops (or the books) to their proper location.

### Move Materials Using the Two-Cart System

When you move whole shelves of materials, you would not want to move one book at a time. You would prefer to move whole shelves, or even cases worth of books, at a time. For this, you will need to use a cart. For efficient slotting, you should employ the **two-cart system**. This means that you will use only two book trucks or carts at a time, and that only two carts of materials will be displaced from the shelves at any given time.

The reason for limiting the movement to only two carts is to avoid the **honeycomb effect**, which is having too many items displaced, stacked up, and taking up floor space. When you remove too many books at once, and you have suffered the honeycomb effect, you'll spend too much time repeatedly moving stacks of displaced books, working to decipher where the piles are supposed to be, and then determining what to move next. Moving piles of books multiple times to get materials where they belong is not just counterproductive for efficiency, but physically demanding. It will also only serve to confuse you and cause you to regret starting the project in the first place.

### *How to Employ the Two-Cart System*

In theory, you could begin at any shelf, but we will begin at what we have designated our best or prime shelf. To reiterate, the best shelf is the one closest to the circulation desk, the front door, or the first one in the area where the highest-circulating items are most accessible and should begin. Now go to the shelves with your two carts:

1. Locate the materials that you want to put on the prime shelf. We'll call those the prime materials.
2. Fill the first cart with the prime materials (and the white label) and take it to the prime shelf (matching the information on the yellow label).
3. From the prime shelf, take the second cart and fill it with the materials (and its white label) that are currently taking space on the prime shelf and let the second cart and books wait there.
4. Empty the prime materials onto the empty prime shelf.
5. Now let the second cart's waiting materials travel to its new location.
6. Repeat the process of removing what is taking up space, placing what belongs there now, and moving the displaced materials to their new location.

Let the displaced contents and their labels of the shelves direct you to the shelf that will be next in line to exchange.

Remember, the white and yellow labels were created at the same time. The yellow labels were collected and then redistributed to mark where the contents of the shelves will be after the reslotting. As you move the contents of the shelves, you will need to remember to keep the white label with the books that are being moved, and that the white labels are traveling to meet back up with the yellow labels that are marking the final destination of the books. When the white and yellow labels are together again, you have successfully relocated the books.

Another layer for consideration is that you won't want to move just one shelf at a time throughout the entire process. One shelf worth of books was used for demonstration purposes and may be the preferred way to transfer materials until you have found the rhythm of the process and have gained confidence in your ability to make the move. But the learning curve is steep, so as you gain experience after two or three shelves have been reslotted, you'll see that you may be able to move an entire bookcase worth of materials at once, especially if you are moving materials from one case of equal height and contents to another. Moving contents from six-foot shelves to three-foot shelves, for example, may take a bit more thought and practice.

As you go through the slotting process, you'll sincerely believe that you should or could be working in order, from the 000s to the 900s—from beginning to end as you bounce back and forth between shelves in what seems like a random order. But rest assured that when you employ the two-cart slotting method, you are employing a technique that has been utilized and refined since the beginning of the industrial revolution, and you are moving items in the most effective way possible. After methodically repeating the process, following the directions of the white and yellow labels, and referring to the plan-o-gram, at some point, you will realize—almost unceremoniously—that all the shelves have emerged in order! When this happens, you may have a few shelves that remain in need of exchange because they are a direct exchange with one another. Scan the room to make sure all white and yellow labels are reunited on the shelf. When they are, you should take some time to celebrate your accomplishment.

### Remember to Employ Safe Materials Handling Practices

Because you will be involved in repetitious and strenuous physical activity, you need to be careful to not overfill the cart so you do not injure yourself by pushing too much weight. Wear closed-toe shoes so you do not trip and fall or injure your feet with rolling wheels or dropped books. Do your best to avoid bending, stooping, or lifting with your back. And always remember to move books entirely within your power zone. Because of all the movement, remember to hydrate frequently. Finally, when it comes to moving heavy shelves, enlist the help of professional movers to relocate the shelves and use the plan-o-gram to show them where you want the shelves to be located.

When the library begins to function in an improved manner with simple reconfiguration of the space, you may soon see evidence that the value to the general public and perhaps your administration also will increase.

## Case Study

Librarians who continue their careers at a new location, or who are new to librarianship, are typically the ones who seem more able to discern that a library is in need of rearrangement or reconfiguration. One librarian observed, "When I first came to this library, I couldn't figure out where to find things. The shelves just didn't make sense. I found the beginning of the fiction books along the wall and made it to the G's, and then poof! The rest of the fiction seemed just gone because the non-fiction books started where the G's left off in the very back of the room. I finally figured out that the fiction continued all the way back at the beginning of the fiction books but on the shelves in the middle of the room. It just was so crazy. I couldn't tell people where to find books because I wasn't sure myself. Plus, everything was getting misplaced. It was a mess and it made me feel like I didn't know what I was doing." If someone has arranged a library in a way that makes sense to them but it doesn't make sense to someone else, the problem is that only the librarian can locate items, and independent searches by students, teachers, or patrons, are hindered by an esoteric organization method.

Sometimes there seems to be no clear reason why it is difficult for students or stakeholders to find what they need. The configuration can make for difficult library visits for the patrons. "Checkout seems really hard for the kids," said another librarian. "They just can't seem to find what they need. They bump into each other, and it takes a long time for them to sit down to other work." Materials that are most popular may have been located in an inconvenient location, and prime space is being wasted on less desirable materials. Sometimes just relocating the more highly circulated materials to a better location will help with the flow of books and other resources.

Also, the placement of the shelves can be problematic. "My aisles are just too long! People are causing trouble in the back and I can't see what they are up to. By the time I realize they are playing around, by the time I get to them, they've run away. The long aisles of shelves keep me from getting to them in time. I'm afraid if I'm not careful, one day somebody is going to get hurt."

After reslotting the books on the shelves, the change can be dramatic. "Wow! It's great to be able to direct people to what they need. Now that the fiction and non-fiction books are located either entirely on the interior shelves or along the wall, the way they flow in a continuous order helps everyone to find and check out, and even return books to the shelves on their own. It's saved me a lot of time because I don't have to keep putting misplaced books back where they belong

*Change #9: Reconfigure the Library Space*

nearly as much as I used to. And putting all the books back, for that matter, is just easier for everyone now."

Placing more desirable materials toward the front of the library and less circulated books toward the back eases the access to and accordingly eases the manner in which people use a library. "My students just really seem calm in the library now. They can browse the shelves very easily. They aren't bumping into each other. They just seem like they are more at peace—enjoying the space. And that makes me enjoy it, too."

Having gaps between cases, instead of long rows, can also have a calming effect. "Because I can get to almost any spot in the library quickly, people don't sneak around in the back so much anymore. I guess they realize that they don't stand a chance if they play around, so it seems like people are more down to business. I like that!"

And how was the moving process? Did you follow the reslotting procedures? "It was really scary at times. I kept moving things and I thought it just couldn't be right. I felt a little confused about it at times, but I kept going. Then just all of a sudden everything was in place. It was weird! But it worked."

"No, I didn't follow the steps. I just pulled everything off the shelves, stacked them on top and on the floor. I just wanted to have empty shelves to fill back up again. It was a lot of work! And it probably took me a lot longer than it should have . . . but oh, well. It's done." There's no harm in doing it this way, and if working a little harder than you need to doesn't bother you, then go for it!

"I just did a little at a time. I wasn't in any hurry, and things were a little confused for a while, but we're there now. And it was worth it." The moral of the story is, there are no reslotting police. Do what is best for you and for the amount of time that you have to spend on the task. The important thing is to consider your stakeholders and their needs and to provide a space that delivers.

## References

"Creating a Slotting Strategy." *Material Handling Management*, vol. 62, no. 3, 2007, pp. 42–43.

Riley, James F., and J. M. Juran. *Process Management*. McGraw-Hill Professional, 1999.

Trevino, S., P. Wutthisirisart, J. Noble, and A. Chang. An approach for order-based warehouse slotting. *IIE Annual Conference Proceedings*, 2009, pp. 569–573.

CHAPTER FOURTEEN

# Change #10: Prepare for Refurnishing, Renovating, Remodeling, or New Construction

As time passes, it may become evident that the library isn't able to keep up with the demands of those it was intended to serve. You'll know this is the case when people express their frustrations or disappointments more frequently. With the rapid rate of technological advances, new devices and resources that require the latest technology to function properly are exciting to use. Also, there are people who rely on a library to gain access because they lack the resources to acquire these items for themselves. In addition to technology, there's constantly changing trends in education in response to political policies and economic trends. With e-books, laptops, and personal devices to access digital materials, space requirements are different. There is more space to enjoy as less space is used for shelving. The wave of demands drive expectations for the types of services people need to receive and, consequently, redefine the library space needed to facilitate those services. Your goal may now be to create a library by refurnishing, renovating, or remodeling it to be functional, fun, comfortable, and appropriately lit.

Other factors that impact the library are environmental and social concerns. A once state-of-the-art library is no longer perceived as a prize if it is an energy waster or if the materials with which it is built are hazardous to people's health. It's also unacceptable if it can't be easily accessed by people with disabilities. Since the library is the place for all people to thrive, grow in knowledge, and improve, public opinion demands that access to the most current resources and methods of accessing those resources, in an environment that is safe for both individuals and the world, is a must. It only stands to reason that a customer service–driven library needs to work hard to meet, as well as it is able, those demands.

If you are questioning how environmental and human concerns impact efficiency and service, then the answer is this: Librarians can spend far too much time trying to accommodate the needs of individuals, then restoring the library to order after furniture or materials have been moved in an effort to grant access to inaccessible things, or apologizing for the space and its shortcomings. Even worse, a librarian may begin to experience health issues caused by the building itself. When you are sick or injured, you are unable to perform your duties to the best of your ability. If this is the case, something needs to be done to remedy the situation.

While Chapter 13 addressed a less costly "do-it-yourself" reconfiguration, a plan to improve an existing space, there may come a time when the help of a professional designer, architect, or engineer will be needed for refurnishing, renovating, or remodeling an existing space or constructing an entirely new space. This chapter introduces information that will help you prepare for major changes in the library. In addition to vocabulary, building code and compliance will be introduced so that you'll know why certain decisions are made when making modifications to an existing structure or when building a new structure. With a basic understanding of these concepts, you'll be better able to communicate your expectations and read architectural plans to understand, recommend, or challenge decisions in an informed way. Additionally, with this background knowledge, you'll be better able to develop the ability to draw on your experience as a librarian and use your "mind's eye" to foresee possible problems in the design of a space or visualize the results of the work.

## Learn the Language to Communicate Your Needs

Successful professionals will agree that speaking to their clients in plain language—without the academic vocabulary or jargon of their profession—is essential. When the goal is to come to a meeting of the minds, avoid misunderstandings, and arrive at a satisfying result for all parties involved, it's best to use plain language to assure that expectations are met. Even if you're fortunate enough to be working with such an astute professional, it's still extremely helpful to acquire an architectural or design vocabulary so that you can communicate your needs for now and

Change #10: Refurnishing, Renovating, Remodeling, or New Construction

in the future, so the communication time is spent collaborating and working toward creating a space that is optimal.

> ### CASE STUDY
>
> A certified architect, who has redesigned library space for schools, explains that it is necessary that he sit down with the client to understand what it is they want from the space. "If I don't do that, then I'm not doing my job. More often than not," he says, "they are hoping to decrease the number of shelves, and increase access to technology and electrical outlets. But the problem is [that] sometimes what they want and trying to make it happen exceeds their budget. This happens because the priority in construction is to make sure the building is safe. And it takes a lot of money to bring old buildings up to code first."

## Degrees of Change

Libraries can experience dramatic improvements by varying degrees of change. After a **reconfiguration** of a library, as discussed in Chapter 13, **refurnishing** with tables, chairs, shelves, or displays may be all that's necessary to achieve the desired update to make a library far more functional than it was before. The least costly of all the projects discussed in this chapter, an existing space can achieve noticeable improvements simply with a purchase of highly functional furniture and fixtures. However, one caveat is that adding or changing furniture without addressing flaws in the layout will not achieve the desired effect. For example, an outdated short wall that was built exclusively to house the electrical wires for desktop computers can take up far too much valuable space. They limit the ability to redesign the space without excessive action such as demolition of the wall, and you will not be able to reach a level of flexibility in the space that is desperately needed.

A **renovation**, however, is a change of the current structure and space. It is the least costly of changes made to a structure, and may provide sufficient improvement in condition and usability. It may include measures such as installing energy-saving windows; replacing old cooling or heating units with more efficient ones; replacing worn flooring, fixtures, or surfaces; and adding electrical outlets. The purpose of a renovation is to make the existing structure like new again without creating additional space.

A **remodel** of an existing structure will include new features that didn't exist before. Adding, extending, or gutting a building to relocate walls and rooms is a remodel. More specifically, examples of library remodeling projects would include removing walls from adjacent rooms to create a larger, open-concept library; adding walls to create smaller conference or study space; moving or increasing the number of restrooms or entry ways for better access; or adding special features such as or outdoor learning and reading areas to create aesthetically pleasing grounds.

**New construction** is the creation of an entirely new structure or addition to a building that will either be put where a building did not exist before or be placed in the same location of an existing building. When there is new construction, even though there is an all-new structure, the possibilities are not limitless. The budget, code, and other factors strongly influence the extent of improvements that can be made to a library.

## Budgetary Factors

A community that values libraries will provide whatever funding it is capable of providing, either from its tax base, bonds, or fundraising. So, whatever the source, there are multiple factors to consider for the wise use of funds dedicated to library improvement projects.

### *Low Budget, High Impact: Shelves, Tables, Seating*

With moderate funds, you can give the library space not just an efficient arrangement but also an updated look by purchasing furniture and fixtures. Flexible space is highly achievable with an addition of movable shelves, movable and stackable tables, and stackable chairs. These items create flexible spaces—extending the life of the library and its ability to adapt to change for years to come.

Consulting an interior designer, or a library furnishings company that offers design services free of charge, can help you make creative changes. Keep in mind that the "free" service is in exchange for purchasing their furniture and equipment. However, there may be approved vendors established by the board of trustees, purchasing department, or another authoritative group. If you discover furnishings that you strongly believe will be the best choice for the space, petition to have that vendor approved. There should be a shared goal of purchasing furniture and light fixtures that last a significant amount of time, so selecting a company that provides the greatest amount of appeal in function, durability, as well as price, is essential.

Other considerations for determining which company to do business with include the length of time it takes to produce and deliver the order, the degree of customer service you will receive during and after delivery including assembly or installation, warranties on material and construction, and the length of time the style or colors will be available—in case there are plans for additional purchases at a later date. If you are able, you may also want to take into consideration the environmental impact of the materials used or the vendor's ethical business practices, but when it comes to budget considerations, making decisions that are practical is always best.

If you purchase furnishings from a catalog or online without a customer service representative visiting with you prior to the purchase, work to establish a friendly, collaborative relationship by phone. It's important to be prepared to ask questions, make requests, and negotiate. You will also want to receive constructive feedback from the representative. Regardless of your budget, the best company which to make major purchases from should be customer service oriented and prepared to do what is reasonably necessary to accommodate your needs, even if they have never seen you in person. The representative should help you understand the products you are interested in purchasing and determine if they'll meet your needs. Also, ask for a clear explanation of the terms of shipment and procedures should you encounter problems. Be certain to have an agreement that payment will be remitted after delivery has been received in full, and to your satisfaction. When the expectations are understood in advance, you will have worked to build a cooperative relationship, and the service representative will work to resolve problems quickly, while minimizing expenses.

You can determine whether a vendor is reliable by asking them for references. Not only will they provide names and contact information, they should also be responsive because they want your business now and in the future. They should also realize that a public space, such as a library, makes an excellent showcase to attract potential clients in the future. So if you begin dealing with a company that is not helpful or does not try to work to earn your trust, sever ties immediately and begin looking for another. If that dealer distributes a manufacturer's product that you want, call the manufacturer directly and ask for another company that sells their product.

### *Electrical Compliance*

With so many devices requiring the use of electricity, one of the first structural modifications that should be addressed is increasing the number of power sources. According to the Electrical Safety Foundation International, buildings constructed prior to 1975 are dramatically out of current code. The code that pertains to the wiring of a building is updated every three years in an effort to ensure safe accommodations of current power needs. While code compliance is only required for newly constructed buildings, not making the effort to update electrical sources in public buildings may be a danger to both the employees and patrons. Temporary measures for providing access to power is not only time consuming every time someone has to drag extension cords from storage, plug them in, and run the line, but they are hazards. They are a potential fire hazard when outlets are overloaded and a tripping hazard when lying across the floor, unnoticed by an unsuspecting passerby. It is best to get an electrical engineer or a licensed electrician to perform an inspection of the wiring. As an option, they can provide a list of required improvements and their cost.

In renovation projects, there are options to increase the number of power sources within the building. Running electricity along the outside of walls, as opposed to within the walls, is known as **surface wiring**. This is a quick alternative to running new wires on the interior of the walls to increase electrical access on the perimeter of the library. To extend power toward the interior of the library, you may wish to inquire if **under-carpet cable installation** is a possibility. Replacing outdated wiring and increasing the number of outlets in the walls and under the flooring are ideal, especially when the building is older and in need of an update. Also, updating with more energy-efficient lighting, and air conditioning and heating, can make electrical circuits available for other uses.

### *International Building Code Compliance*

If there are larger funds available, perhaps construction projects are a possibility. Know that all construction is subject to the rules and constraints of the building code as adopted by the **Authorities Having Jurisdiction** (AHJ). The AHJ is the agency that regulates all construction locally. There are several versions of code to be followed, determined by geographic regions in the United States; and because code can be modified at the local level, it varies from state to state, municipality to municipality. However, regardless of the jurisdiction or the code utilized, most all code is an adaptation of the **International Building Code** (IBC) as developed by the International Code Council.

Building code is intended to ensure safety and accessibility of anyone who inhabits a space. So this may mean that grand ideas or visions could be limited by factors such as the number of people who will occupy the space, existing structures in the surrounding areas, the land or geography, among others. For example, the hope for a multi-floored public library to be built with a cafe that prepares hot food, or a school library with an atrium in the center, may not be feasible because of costs associated with controlling or minimizing fire hazards.

## Americans with Disabilities Act Compliance

The next thing to consider with renovations is that it may be necessary to reserve funds to first meet federal requirements for compliance with the Americans with Disabilities Act (ADA of 1990).

When a construction project is budgeted at $50,000 or more, a plan review and inspection are required by authorized ADA services. The AHJ cannot modify this requirement at a local level because it is not code, it is law. Laws are enforceable by legal action through the courts.

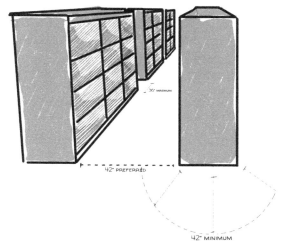

**Figure 14.1** Distances between Shelves That Provide Accessibility

Even if the project budget does not exceed the threshold, when it is "readily achievable," budget allocations should still be made to accommodate impairments such as mobility, hearing, vision, speech, cognitive, short stature, and limited mobility (for people not necessarily requiring the use of a wheelchair). Providers of public space want to be in compliance with ADA, so in addition to meeting building accessibility requirements, from the librarian's perspective, it's good to think ahead about possible obstructions to accessibility at key locations in the library including the circulation desk, the space between the shelves, seating areas, as well as location and availability of electrical outlets. Figure 14.1 shows the amount of clearance needed between furnishings so that a person in a wheelchair is able to pass through the space as easily as possible.

## Environmental Rating Systems

Leadership in Energy and Environmental Design (LEED), developed by the U.S. Green Building Council (USGBC), outlines a series of options that can be selected by the municipality or governmental organization and design team that serve as a raised "ceiling" for practice in constructing a building that is environmentally friendly and reduces the carbon footprint of the library space. According to LEED, "buildings have a substantial impact on the health and well-being of people and the planet. Buildings use resources, generate waste and are costly to maintain and operate. **Green building** is the practice of designing, constructing, and operating buildings to maximize occupant health and productivity, use fewer resources, reduce waste and negative environmental impacts, and decrease life cycle costs." Utilizing LEED specifications is not code compliance. It's a recognition that the building is a healthier indoor space; uses lower amounts of energy, water, and other resources; and makes the statement that the building is better for the occupants, the community, and the environment. Communities with LEED recognition inspire feelings of pride and ownership in the space for the people it serves and establish that the municipality is an environmental leader.

## Blueprints, Architectural Sheets, or Construction Drawings

When reconfiguring, updating, remodeling an existing or constructing a new building, it is imperative to have access to and an ability to read architectural sheets or construction drawings. "Blueprints" was the term once used for the technical drawings associated with construction. According to the American Institute of Architecture, **blueprints** "show in graphic and quantitative form the extent, design, location, relationships, and dimensions of the work to be done . . . and generally contain site and building plans, elevations, sections, details, schedules, and diagrams."

Historically, blueprints were white, but the chemical process used on the paper turned the paper blue! In contemporary architecture, the terms **sheets** or **construction drawings** should be used in lieu of "blueprints." You may find construction drawings printed on any size paper, but 18×24, 24×36, and 42×30 are typically used.

Figure 14.2 shows blueprints that were created in the late 1950s that measured 3 feet by 19 inches, and also sheets from 2010s that are printed on letter- and legal-sized paper. Sheets for large construction projects, such as a school campus, are very large and unwieldly. When you have sheets such as these, it is imperative use great care when handling them. Large-sized sheets should be rolled facing out to carry and store so when used, the paper will lay flat. All prints, however, should be protected when not being used and stored in a clean, dry location. You should also avoid writing, placing beverages, or placing sharp objects on them.

How the construction drawings are organized will vary, and sometimes the names of key plans vary as well. In order to read and understand them, you will need the **title page**. The title page, which is similar to the table of contents of a book and the legend of a map, outlines the

Change #10: Refurnishing, Renovating, Remodeling, or New Construction 149

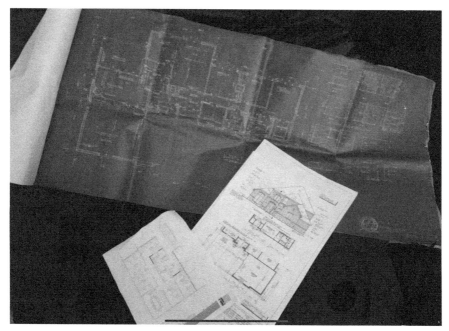

**Figure 14.2** Blueprints and Other Construction Sheets

order of the drawings and provides a page number and brief description of all the sheets. It also defines the symbols used throughout the set of plans. If you are offered a copy of the library plan, be certain to ask for the title page as well so you can get familiar with and understand the details of the drawing and the building.

The types of drawings that you will see in a set of sheets, in addition to the title page, are the civil, structural, architectural, as well as the mechanical, plumbing, and electrical plans (collectively known as the MPE).

Table 14.1 outlines the terminology that you will find on key architectural plan pages and describes the type of information they contain.

### Advice for Individuals Who Are Participating in a Renovation or New Construction

Getting involved in the planning and decision-making of a renovation or new construction project may be difficult, but it is not impossible.

You may be asking yourself: If there is ever construction or renovation in my future, and I take the time to learn all this information, what is the possibility that I will actually be involved in the project? At times, the opinions of the librarians may be asked, but then when the construction commences, it becomes quite evident that none of the

**Table 14.1 Arrangement of Drawing Sets, Sheets, or Construction Drawings: All the Information They Contain**

| | |
|---|---|
| Cover Sheet | Project name and client, architect, engineers, and special consultants |
| Index and General Information Sheet | List of Drawings |
| | General Notes, Advance Requirements, etc. |
| | Project Location Map (can be in the state, city, or general vicinity) |
| Code Information | Life Safety Plan(s) |
| Additional Information (small projects) | Floor area, exit pathways, lists of stored items essential to the building department plan reviewers |
| Civil | Site Plan: Civil engineer's drawings to show earthwork, utilities, fire truck lanes, fencing, property lines, easements, lot and block designations, zoning, etc. |
| Architectural | Demolition Drawings: Floor plans, elevations, sections and details that convey all demolition that will occur per the following list of drawings for construction |
| | Site Plan: Parking, signs, sidewalks, trees, kiosks, other freestanding structures in the project, etc. |
| | Floor Plans: Include interior walls, doors, windows as well as all that is connected to the building's exterior |
| | Ceiling Plans: Lights, mechanical devices, audio visual equipment, etc. |
| | Roof Plan: Roof material, slopes, and equipment |
| | Schedules: Identify the room finish materials, color, and equipment manufacturers and models as well as performance requirements |
| | Building Elevations: Show exterior walls, lights, materials, windows, etc. |
| | Building Sections: Show a cut through the entire building, may also be for portions of the building but always to convey the floor-to-floor heights and overall height of the work |
| | Wall Sections and Details: Show wall materials, thicknesses, and the extent of hidden materials within the wall |

*(continued)*

**Table 14.1** (continued)

| | |
|---|---|
| | Enlarged Floor Plans and Details: Rooms with special equipment and accessories are enlarged and noted to identify the special equipment and accessories. Plan views typical and atypical wall corners are shown here, too. |
| | Special Systems: Any additional special equipment designed by the architect is provided here. |
| Structural | General Information Sheet: Structural typically identifies standard and special requirements of the project here. |
| | Drawings for demolition and construction are typically arranged like architectural plans. |
| MEP (Mechanical, Electrical, Plumbing) | General Information Sheet: Each discipline provides a sheet of abbreviations and symbols to understand the contents of the drawing sheets to follow. |
| Special Systems | These can include drawings provided by acoustic specialists, audiovisual designers, and kitchen equipment. |

recommendations were taken into consideration. Additionally, between the creation of the architectural plans, the engineering interpretation, and then the actual construction, so much can vary. Details or preferences may be lost when the budget dictates which materials or special features get left out.

But most often, the space that is created for a library, as part of a larger project, is simply a square, something that is essentially a warehouse. A warehouse for books, and a space for people to gather, research, learn, seek entertainment, or just be.

---

### Case Study

School librarian Carolyn Foote, from Westlake High School in Austin, Texas, was presented with the opportunity of being the librarian in charge during the renovation of an existing library and she decided she was going to make herself available to meet with the construction team. "[Even though] I was invited, [I still] felt I was being overrun by some of the subcontractors. So, I wrote up an agenda and printed it out before every meeting to assure [that] our needs were heard." This is excellent advice for keeping your needs and ideas for solutions in the forefront of the discussion.

Did the contractors take into consideration all her suggestions? She stated that some of the features, such as sliding glass doors on some small group meeting rooms, were used. "That was my idea!" She also expressed that the library was being used as a passthrough for students to get from one class to another. After informing the contractors that this activity was a problem because it was disruptive in the library, the contractors came up with the solution of making a glass enclosed hallway. "I lost some space, but it was worth it to me to not have all of the noise and distraction."

By this librarian participating in the planning process of construction, being determined to make her voice heard, the library better serves the needs of the students and facilitates the operations of the library.

Wilson County Public Library is located in a rural Texas town called Floresville. It was once housed in a small building in the center of town, but was later moved into a significantly larger, renovated school building. The librarian and director, Nicki Stohr, stated, "I was involved in all the meetings. It was a long process that took several years. We started in 2012 and we moved into the new building in 2016. It started with a lot of surveys to see what patrons wanted. [One major thing the staff and I] discovered was that the noise of story time impacted the adults and their usage of the computers. [We were made aware that the children's programming] was so noisy that we knew that the lab would have to be enclosed, and the children's area would have to be as far away from the lab as possible. Now, they are in opposite parts of the library."

By staying very involved in the planning process, "we got everything we asked for. The only thing we did not get was a coffee bar! We even had one staff member who was ready to go to barista school, but the county commissioners said they were not interested in getting into the restaurant business! But we came up with an easy solution. We got a vending machine!"

When moving to the newly renovated building, the library divested itself of its large, cherished collection of historical photos and books. "We asked that the old building be kept and made into a town historical archive. [The commissioners agreed and] moved the archive into the original county library—which had been part of the old jail house. The archive is now managed by a part-time archivist and lots of enthusiastic volunteers!"

For the new building, she said, "we [asked for] space for the adults, for kids, a makerspace, a separate computer lab, and separate office area. Our target audience is not narrow so we had to encompass everybody, ages zero to 99 plus. Our oldest patron comes to visit almost every week. He just turned 100! He tells us, 'I'm here to make sure you're doin' it right!' Our children have an enclosed story time area where they can shut the door, be really loud, and have fun! We feel there is a little something for everyone, and that's exactly what we were looking for!"

What has this done for attendance? "For last May, June, and July, each month the door count was over 10,000 people! For a rural county library, we are so busy! Two to three times a day, Monday through Friday, something is going on." But because funds are limited and staffing is costly, the number of staff has not increased. "Because we grew in size but not number of staff, we went RFID. We have a new self-check station." A staff member is kept near the front desk to help if people are blocked from checkout for some reason, but before, in the old building with a staff member checking out, the line could form that was as long as the entire width of the building. Now, with self-check, "even sloppy stacks can be checked out fast, all at once."

The fact that this librarian was able to get so much support from the county officials is significant. When asked if the commissioners really value libraries as much as it appears that they do, she stated very enthusiastically, "We have a wonderful support system when it comes to the politicians in the city. All I have to do is ask, but I keep it within reason by not asking for the world. I knew that the friends of the library wanted a new location. When we started looking for a building, the school district put the property on the market, and the county bought the property. The library is supported with an ad valorem tax: a portion of the property taxes go to the library. The county commissioners offered the old school building for the new library and the renovation costs were included in a bond." Did the bond pass with flying colors?

"No, actually. Just barely. This is a rural community [and money is tight.] But it wasn't until we moved into the new building that we went from being small, dark, and dingy to a spread-out, airy, and bright library that so many people come to enjoy. It's just like offering food! Free food brings everybody. Doesn't it?"

## References

"Blueprint Fundamentals." YouTube, Feb. 4, 2016. www.youtube.com/watch?v=5uBTzoe9Pvs&feature=youtu.be

Ching, Francis D. K., and Steven R. Winkel. *Building Codes Illustrated: A Guide to Understanding the 2018 International Building Code.* Wiley, 2018.

CommScope. "Undercarpet Cabling Installation." YouTube, Jan. 22, 2016. www.youtube.com/watch?v=9WcnxlhxsKk

"ESFI: The National Electrical Code—2020." Electrical Safety Foundation International, www.esfi.org/resource/the-2020-national-electrical-code-594

Griffin, Peter. "The Rate of Technological Change Is Now Exceeding Our Ability to Adapt." Noted, May 24, 2018. www.noted.co.nz/tech/the-rate-of-technological-change-is-now-exceeding-our-ability-to-adapt/

"The International Building Code." ICC, Feb. 19, 2019. www.iccsafe.org/products-and-services/i-codes/2018-i-codes/ibc/

"Introduction to Print Reading—Drawing Organization—Lines & Symbols." YouTube, Aug. 5, 2013. www.youtube.com/watch?v=gKJjjGNJ5cs&feature=youtu.be

"LEED Rating System." USGBC, new.usgbc.org/leed

Roser, Max, and Hannah Ritchie. "Technological Progress." Our World in Data, ourworldindata.org/technological-progress

Russell, Ron. *Print and Specifications Reading for Construction*. Wiley, 2011.

United States Access Board. "Chapter 4: Accessible Routes." www.access-board.gov/guidelines-and-standards/buildings-and-sites/about-the-ada-standards/ada-standards/chapter-4-accessible-routes#401 General

# Conclusion

Arriving at a conclusion for a book that is about process management in the library is somewhat impossible. This is because process management is never really complete—it is a continuing event. Process management is an ongoing, self-assessing, ever-evolving practice of evaluating and reevaluating and striving to meet inevitable change head-on with a plan.

It doesn't really matter what has brought you to read this book. You could have recently begun a new job at a library, chosen to adopt the routine of your predecessor, assessed the situation, and concluded that changes had to be made to suit your needs and philosophy of the type of library service that you want to provide. Or you might have been at the same library for years, and over time, you have discovered that your own routines have become ineffective and in need of improvement. The important fact is that you decided that now is the time to make some changes and you have taken matters into your own hands.

Time has a habit of changing technology that forces us to stop and learn and adapt and utilize newly evolved hardware and software as tools and access points to information. Time also causes expectations of and demands on the librarian to change, as well. As long as you serve the public, there will always come a time and impetus for the need to adjust and improve.

Change that is imposed on you is inevitable. When faced with change imposed by any reason other than your own, you will have only two choices:

1. Resist and get left behind, or
2. Embrace and adjust and lead the charge.

The 10 simple changes that you can implement to improve library service will help you continue to observe, analyze, troubleshoot, and improve on your situation now and in the future. But as simple as these steps are, they also take time to implement. So remember to start from the beginning, be patient with yourself, and be prepared to revisit the same processes and ways to improve them as many times as necessary. You may not be able, or find the opportunity, to address all of these changes, but any small or big one that you choose to implement can help you overcome the obstacles and give you the opportunity to work in the happiest and healthiest manner that you can. Any change will allow you, in turn, to provide the very best service that your patrons deserve.

I congratulate you on your desire to work to improve everything that is within your control, and your willingness to take control of what may have seemed out of reach. I firmly believe that every librarian who strives to be successful at what they do does so much to remind the world that libraries are an indispensable part of the community that they serve, and that they keep this profession alive and essential in even the most trying of times. I wish you much success in your efforts as a librarian, those of you who have chosen to live a life serving others in this very fine and noble profession.

# Index

Note: Page numbers in *italic* indicate figures; page numbers in **bold** refer to tables.

academic librarians, 23
accounting controls, 67–70
accounting journals, 69–70
acquisitions, 24
American Library Association, 22
Americans with Disabilities Act (ADA) compliance, 147
architectural sheets, 148–149, **150–151**
audit trail, 72, 78
auditors, 69

bar coding, 83
Barrera, Gilbert C., Jr., 77–78
blueprints, 124, 148–149, *149*, **150–151**
bookkeeping records, 75
books
    checking in, 5, 7, 16, 53, 59, 61–62
    checking out, 16
    on desk, 34
    shelving, 5, 7, 17, 59–61
    staging, 7
Boyes, Alice, 4
budget plans, 7
budgetary factors
    Americans with Disabilities Act (ADA) compliance, 147

electrical compliance, 145–146
environmental rating systems, 147–148
International Building Code (IBC) compliance, 146
shelves, tables, seating, 144–145

carbon footprint, 147
carpal tunnel syndrome, 111
cataloging, 24
checking in books, 5, 7, 16, 53, 59, 61–62
    self-check-in station, 62–63
checking out books, 16
circulation, 50–51
circulation desk, 12, 30, 37–38
    analysis of circulation desk processes, 56, **57**, 58–59
    expanded analysis of processes, **54–55**
    identifying essential activities, **52**
    working away from, 89
closing routines, 40–41
collaboration, 19, 25
collection development, 16, 18, 23
collection management, 15–16, 23. *See also* weeding

communication
  answering in-person reference questions, 89–91
  answering phone reference questions, 91–92
  answering the phone, 90–91
  effective procedures for, 87–95
  handling e-mails, 92–93
  managers with poor skills, 103–104, 106
  in school libraries, 93–95
  working away from the desk, 89
community outreach, 25
construction drawings, 148–149, **150–151**
construction plans, 124
construction sheets, *149*
continuous review evaluation weeding (CREW), 117
customer satisfaction, 51
customer service, 18, 92
  improving, 14, 18, 56, 65, 101
  negative experiences, 89
  as priority, 12, 40, 51, 82, 87–88, 95, 142
  from vendors, 13, 24, 144–145

daily routines, 39–40
  analysis of circulation desk processes, 56, **57**, 58–59
  circulation, 50–51
  gathering reports, 48–50
  material returns, 62–63
  modifying small problems, 62
  nonrecurring events, 63
  opening and closing, 40–41
  planning phase, 51–53
  practice exercise, 41–45
  preopening routines, 45–48
  proper location of tools, supplies, and people, 63
  selecting one process in the planning phase, 53, 56
  shelving books, 59, 60–62
  sorting materials, 59–60
  steps taken in morning routine, **42–43**
decluttering, 115–117
desk reorganization
  arranging books, 34
  arranging everything else, 36–37
  arranging papers, 35
  arranging personal items, 35
  daily clean-up, 36–37
  gaining a new perspective, 29–30
  identifying tasks, 30–31
  preparing an action plan, 30
  sorting items by type, 33–34
  tools, resources, and space, 31–33
digital resources, 22
documentation of purchases, 71–72

efficiency, 11
  and desk reorganization, 36
  effect of stress on, 101
  fears and misconceptions about, 15–19
  in handling emails, 92–93
  need for adequate space, 32
  NIOSH recommendations to improve, **113**
  in time management, 25–26
  *See also* time management
electrical compliance, 146
e-mails, 92–93
  auto-response messages, 93
  processing requests through, 94–95
  templates for, 93
emergency situations, 94–95
encumbrances, 69
environmental rating systems, 147–148
expenditures, 68–69

Farris, Paul, 51
fiduciary relationships, 66

goodwill, 19, 33
growth plan, 10, 13–14
  self-directed, 14

injury prevention, 112–113
interior design, 144–145
International Building Code (IBC) compliance, 146
interpersonal relationships, 113
invoices, 74–75

jacket cover dispenser, 85–86
Janus, Donovan, 75
job enlargement, 111
job rotation, 111
job satisfaction, 18
  and stress, 101
job stress, 101–105. *See also* stressors

label protectors, 83–84
Leadership in Energy and Environmental Design (LEED), 147–148
learning
  collaborative, 19
  individual, 19
  lifelong, 9
  outdoor, 144
  professional, 17–18, 112
  student, 31
lesson plans, 7
librarians
  academic, 23
  reference, 22
  school, 23, 89
library space
  reconfiguring, 123–137
  weeding and clearing, 115–120
lifelong learning, 9
list, quote, or cart, 72
LISTSERV, 22

MAchine Readable Cataloging (MARC), 24
makerspace areas, 12, 13, 37, 38, 46, 98, 110, 116, 152
management skills, 106
managing continuing resources, 24–25

materials handling, 107–110
  carrying, 109
  importance of, 108
  lifting, 108–109
  recommendations, 108–110
  safe practices in reslotting, 137
  using dolly or cart, 110, *110*
  using equipment, 109–110
MUSTY (MUSTI) rule, 117

National Institute for Occupational Safety and Health (NIOSH), 102
  on job stress, 102
  materials handling guidelines, 108
  recommendations to improve safety and efficiency, **113**
new construction, 144
nonrecurring events, 63
nonroutine events, 50

obstacles, 5
Occupational Safety and Health Administration (OSHA), 103, 111
opening routines, 40–41
  steps taken in morning routine, **42–43**
  streamlining process, 44–45
organization, 12, 14, 17
  of desk, 29–38
  of periodicals, 25
  of purchasing documents, 68

packing slips, 73–74
papers on desk, 35
partnership with teachers, 25
patron assistance, 5
patron priorities
  aligning precepts with, 129
  constructing a survey, 125, **126–127**, 127–128
  using to refine plans, 128–129
periodicals, 24–25
petty cash fund, 70
plan-o-gram, 133

preopening routines, 45–47
  beginning to analyze, 46–47
  document process, 45
  evaluating remedies, 47–48
  mapping out tasks, 45–46
  turning on equipment, 47
price negotiation, 24
process decomposition, 56
process management, 10–11, 31, 51
processing station, 30, 81–82
  bar coding, 83
  completing, 86
  efficient use of space, 86
  jacket cover dispenser, 85–86
  justification for, 82
  location and supplies, 82
  processing procedure, 82–83
  property stamp, 84
  radio frequency identification, 84–85
  spine labels and label protectors, 83–84
professional development, 17–18, 22
professional organizations, 22
program planning, 25
property stamps, 84
purchase orders, 70, 73
purchasing, 24
  accounting controls, 65–70
  checklist, **76**
  documenting, 71–72
  formal processes, 71
  fund management, 66
  informal processes, 71
  invoice, 74–75
  keeping records (case study), 77–78
  list, quote, or cart, 72–73
  maintaining records, 75
  organization of purchasing documents, 68
  packing slip, 73–74
  purchase order, 73
  purchasing process, 70–71
  requisition, 73
purchasing space, 66–67

radio frequency identification (RFID), 84–85
receiving. *See* processing station
receiving materials, 76–77
reconfiguration, 143
reconfiguring space, 5, 11
  advice for, 149, 151
  aligning precepts with patron needs, 129
  budgetary factors, 144–148
  building a case for change, 124–125
  case studies, 11–13, 138–139, 151–153
  communicating needs, 142–143
  constructing a survey, 125–128
  degrees of change, 143–144
  finalizing the plan-o-gram, 135
  locating blueprints, 124
  moving materials using two-cart system, 135–137
  new construction, 144
  planning the move, 130
  plans for, 148–149, **150–151**
  reasons for, 141–142
  reconfiguring the shelves, 134
  redistributing shelf labels, 135
  refining plans with patron needs in mind, 128–129
  relocating collections or sections of books, 131–134
  shifting contents of shelves, 130–131
  use safe material handling practices, 137
reference and instruction, 22–23
reference desk, working away from, 89
reference librarians, 22
reference questions, 5, 11
  in-person, 89–91
  phone, 91–92
remodeling, 143–144
renovation, 143
reorder point, 98–100, **99**

# Index

reordering, 98–100
repair. *See* processing station
requisitions, 70, 73
reslotting, 131–133, 134
   preparation for, 133–134
   redistributing shelf labels, 135
   using two-cart system, 135–137
Riley, James, 10, 51

safety stock, 98
school librarians, 23, 89
school libraries
   in person, phone, and e-mail communication, 93–95
   spatial requirements, 129
   special considerations for, 119–120
shelving books, 5, 7, 17, 59
   staging, 61
   technique to expedite, 60–61
sorting materials, 59–60
spine labels, 83–84
staging books, 7
statistics gathering, 48–50
   attendance, 49–50
storage of supplies, 97–98
storage space, decluttering, 116
stress. *See* job stress; stressors
stress management, 103
stressors, 4, 12
   effect on efficiency, 101
   and job satisfaction, 101
   managerial communication skills, 106
   poorly designed tasks, 106–113
   process for eliminating, 105–106
   and workplace health and safety, 102–105
supplies
   location of, 63
   reordering, 98–100
   safety stock, 98
   storage of, 97–98
   storage of supplies, 97–98

tally counter, 48, *49*
task design
   engineering improvements, 107
   ergonomic improvements, 107
   handling tasks administratively, 110–111
   manual materials handling, 107–110
   problems with, 103–104
   sedentary tasks, 111–112
task modification, 6
   postponing tasks, 15–16
task overload, 4
teachers, partnership with, 25
time management, 3–6, 19, 21–22, 95
   acquisitions, 24
   cataloging, 24
   collection development and management, 23
   managing continuing resources, 24–25
   more efficiency, 25–26
   program planning and collaboration, 25
   reference and instruction, 22–23
   *See also* efficiency
title page, 148
two-cart system, 135–137

U.S. Green Building Council (USGBC), 147

weeding
   continuous review evaluation weeding (CREW), 117
   degrees of, 117–119
   keeping outdated materials, 119
   of the library collection, 117
   special considerations for school libraries, 119–120
work environment
   improving, 5–6
   and job satisfaction, 18
   toxic, 103–105, 112–113

work roles
  causing uncertainty, 103
  uncertainty in, 103–104, 112–113
workload issues, 3–6
  case study, 6–7

workplace health and safety, 102–105
workspace, personal vs. nonpersonal, 37–38. *See also* desk reorganization

About the Author

**Elizabeth Barrera Rush**, MSIS, has worked in a variety of library settings including private and public schools, public, and special libraries over the course of 20 years and for the past 3 years as a library support specialist in the Library and Textbook Services Department at Northside Independent School District, San Antonio, Texas. She has also worked as an independent contractor for public and charter schools. She earned her bachelor's degree in business administration at St. Mary's University and her MSIS at the University of Texas at Austin. She is the author of the book *Bringing Genius Hour to Your Library: Implementing a Schoolwide Passion Project Program*, a member of the American Library Association and the Texas Library Association, and an ALA Spectrum Scholar and Champion.